REAL MEN WORK
IN THE
PITS

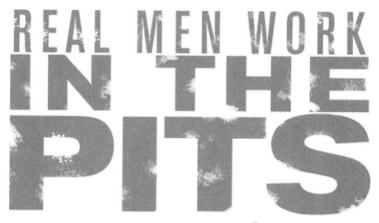

REAL MEN WORK IN THE PITS

A LIFE IN NASCAR® RACING

JEFF HAMMOND

Printed in the United States of America

Rodale Inc. makes every effort to use acid-free ⊗, recycled paper ☺.

Book design by Chris Rhoads

Photographs courtesy of Jeff Hammond's personal collection

NASCAR is a registered trademark of National Association for Stock Car Auto Racing, Inc.

Library of Congress Cataloging-in-Publication Data

Hammond, Jeff.
    Real men work in the pits : a life in NASCAR racing / Jeff Hammond.
        p.   cm.
    Includes index.
    ISBN-13 978–1–59486–161–1 hardcover
    ISBN-10 1–59486–161–7 hardcover
    1. Hammond, Jeff.   2. Pit crew chiefs—United States—Biography.   3. NASCAR
(Association)—History.   I. Title.
    GV1032.H25A3   2005
    796.72—dc22   2004022478

Distributed to the trade by Holtzbrinck Publishers

    4   6   8   10   9   7   5   3   hardcover

With appreciation and love, I dedicate this book
to the special people in my life—

To my parents, Jacque and Nancy: My success is built on
your unconditional love and support. Dad, every day I miss
you . . . and Mom, amid all the chaos that is my life, you are my rock.

To Sharon: Thank you for understanding and supporting me
when times were good and especially when they were not so good.

To Colt: With pride, I have watched my little cowboy
become a strong, handsome young man.
You are my firstborn and my greatest joy.

To beautiful Heather Marie: You are the sparkle in my eye
and, whether you like it or not, you will always be your
daddy's little girl.

And to Jacob: You have so much talent, little man. You are a
gift to me, and I am proud to call you my son.

I am blessed to have each of you be a part of my life.

—JLH

CONTENTS

CONTENTS

1

ACKNOWLEDGMENTS

You don't win in racing on your own. As any reader of this book will see pretty quickly. Success is a team thing. I've learned that this is true in most of the things you do in life, and you need to recognize the people who've been part of your team and thank them. I hope I haven't left anyone who helped me along in my racing career out of these pages. There were so many, though, I may have, and I apologize for it. I've had a lot of help in my second career—broadcasting—and I need to say thanks to: Ed Goren, David Hill, Neil Goldberg, Artie Kempner, Richie Z., Pam Miller, Larry McReynolds, and Chris Myers along with the rest of my Fox family.

This book is the story of my life, but I had help on it and I'd like to thank Van Colley and Danny Shull for reading the manuscript and keeping me straight. And the folks at ICM and Rodale who made it happen and did such a professional job.

Most of all, I'd like to thank my family and friends for everything. Without them, none of the rest of it happens.

When I was a kid, if the wind was right, we could hear them running at the Charlotte Speedway from the house where we lived. I used to listen to that sound and to the announcers on the radio describing the races and calling the names of my favorite drivers—people like Junior Johnson, Lee Petty, and Fireball Roberts. The first race I ever went to at the Speedway was in 1964, and that was the

race where Junior and Ned Jarrett crashed in the back straight and Fireball Roberts wrecked and got burned so badly that he eventually died. I'd been a Roberts fan. After that, I started following Lee Petty's son, Richard.

I remember it wasn't long after that when one Saturday morning my uncle, Brad Tadlock, came over and woke me up and said, "Get out of bed and come with me to pick up a race car." I was 12 years old then, and I never dreamed that this was the beginning of a career—a whole life—in racing.

We went down to Lancaster, South Carolina, and picked up a '56 Ford that was painted school-bus yellow with the number "54" on it. We joked about *Car 54, Where Are You?* which was the big television comedy show back then.

So we brought the car back and changed the number and the paint scheme on it, and my uncle used to run that car at the local short tracks. My deal with my folks was that I'd go to school in the daytime, and then at night, I'd come home and help my uncle work on that car in an open carport right next to our house. My brother, Rodney, who was younger would work with me, and sometimes my dad, Jacque, would pitch in. I'd wash the car, beat the dents out, and do all the mechanical work I could do for the size I was. My uncle and dad called me "Smokey," after Smokey Yunick, a famous car builder. In those days, we were doing everything shade-tree-mechanic style. We had timing lights, but that was about it. No dynos or anything. You worked on that engine by sound and by feel until you got it right. That was the beginning of my education in racing.

After a while, my dad asked my brother and me if we wanted to build our own race car. Well, you can imagine how we took to that. We went to a junkyard and bought an old '56 Ford chassis and a body off a '65 Ford Falcon. My dad was a contractor, so he closed in the carport behind the house to make a garage, and we were in business, building race cars. I learned how to port and polish heads. I also learned how to weld and do the other things that were necessary to build a race car. Once the car was ready, we went out and ran at the local dirt tracks like the Starlight Speedway in Monroe, North Carolina, and the Metrolina in Charlotte. These were the minor leagues of stock car racing, and it was places like that where the great drivers of those days got their starts.

We did pretty good, too. Won some races with a guy named Gene Madry driving for us. The competition was pretty strong in those days. Ralph Earnhardt was still driving. He had one of the better frame machines around in those days, and he straightened our chassis for us after we'd wrecked. There was one time when Dale Earnhardt—who was running dirt tracks back then—came really close to driving for us.

If you knew Ralph back then, you could see where Dale got his personality and his style of driving. I remember Ralph saying that if somebody did something to you in a race, you didn't just do it back to him. You did it back twice as hard. That way you got respect, and the guy didn't mess with you again. You didn't bluff, and you didn't let yourself be bluffed. I believe that's where Dale learned to be the Intimidator—from his father, who was racing on dirt tracks around Charlotte, sometimes against our car.

So it was a great way to learn racing, right there at the roots, and I suspect that it's why I feel the way I do about some of the things I see in racing today. NASCAR, as everybody knows, has come a long, long way. And the sport just keeps getting bigger and bigger, appealing to a wider and wider audience. There weren't many races on television back when I started, and now I'm working for FOX, broadcasting about racing every week and covering the races live. Millions of people watch those broadcasts, and the people who follow racing don't just come from the South anymore.

NASCAR has become national and even international, and I have mixed feelings about that. I believe that sometimes, when it reaches out to new fans and new markets, the sport risks losing touch with its roots. NASCAR is moving races from some of the old, classic short tracks like Rockingham and putting them in places where we've never raced before, like Chicago and Las Vegas. One of the great traditions of racing was the Labor Day race at Darlington, the first superspeedway, and now NASCAR has done away with that. I know growth is a good thing but so is history and tradition, and we don't want to forget what has made our sport great.

A lot has changed since I was in high school learning about the world of racing. Some of these changes are good, and some are not so good. Nobody is a bigger fan and supporter of racing than I am, but when I think NASCAR is making a mistake, I'm going to say so. I love the sport too much not to.

A lot of kids, when they think about racing, want to drive. I wanted to myself, but there was always one thing standing in my way—my mother. She didn't want me to drive, and I had to respect that. My dad would let me take the cars out on the track before a race and warm them up. And later, after I graduated from high school, I did drive a little. But there was a time, somewhere along the way when I was 15 or 16 years old, that I realized that I was pretty good at working on cars and that I loved doing it and what I really wanted to do was be part of a pit crew. I wanted to be one of the guys jumping over the wall and changing tires or working the jack. That, to me, was really exciting.

I got my opportunity to experience what it is like, working in the pits, from meeting Winston Cup drivers at a place called Tiger Tom Pistone's, where we bought parts. The drivers were always coming in and out, and if they heard about how you were pretty good on the dirt tracks, they'd tell you to come over and help out when they were running on the asphalt. Back then, a lot of those guys didn't have regular, full-time pit crews. So you'd get an offer to work from people like Elmo Langley, Frank Warren, Tommy VanDiver, and Walter Ballard, who was probably the guy who helped me most in those early days.

Those guys were all racing legends, and they gave people like me the chance to be part of racing at that level. If you were good, you'd get asked again, and your name would get around, and that's the way it happened for me. I started going around to nearby tracks like Bristol, Rockingham, and Martinsville on the weekends and working for different drivers in the pits. Sometimes there wouldn't be enough people like me for every driver to have his own crew, so we'd make agreements to take two cars. The driver in the lead would come in first to pit, and then the one that was behind would take his turn. You stayed pretty busy, but it was a great way to learn racing. I worked for some good drivers like CooCoo Marlin whose son, Sterling, is one of the NASCAR stars today.

I was starting to think that this was the life I wanted, but the security wasn't there. When I'd get an offer to come to work for someone's crew, I'd talk to my dad about it, and he'd say, "No, hold off a while." He wasn't against my going into racing full-time; he just wanted to make sure I waited for the right opportunity.

I'd gotten to know Herb Nab, who was crew chief for Cale Yarborough. Their team owner was Junior Johnson. Cale and Junior were two of the biggest names in racing. They were legends, especially Junior, who had been a great, natural driver before he got out of the cockpit. And then Junior was just as successful as a team owner, and one of the few who actually made any real money at it. In racing at that time, there wasn't a bigger star than Junior Johnson.

So when Herb Nab, who worked for Junior, asked me before the Darlington race in 1976 if I could weld, I said, "Sure, I can weld."

"What else can you do?"

"Well," I said, "I can do a little body work. Change tires. Sweep floors. And I can *learn* how to do anything I need to do. What are you looking for?"

"I'm looking for somebody who will do anything I tell him to do," Herb said

"Well, I'm your man, Herb," I said.

"Then be at the shop, ready to work, first thing Monday morning, and we'll talk about a job."

I can still remember the way I felt, going home after the race at Darlington. It was a real case of mixed emotions. I was excited and happy to be with the best team in racing but sad to be leaving my dad and the things we'd done together. I woke him up that night and told him.

My dad listened to what I had to say, and then he said, "Make me proud."

I left the next morning for Junior's shop and didn't leave for 10 years.

Junior's shop was in a place called Ronda, North Carolina. That was the mailing address. The actual location of the shop was Engle Hollow. Everybody who worked there said we were graduates of the University of Ronda at Engle Hollow. Junior Johnson was already a legend, and Cale Yarborough was on his way to winning his first championship. So I got in on the last of that. I was the new man and just out of high school, so I was still pretty young. I guess you could say I started at the bottom of the top, sweeping floors and doing whatever needed doing for the best team in racing.

You talk about a dream come true.

I was working there with guys like Bobby Ross and Turkey Minton—who used to change tires for Junior—and Henry Benfield—a racing legend, who was the gas man. They had a lot of colorful people, and I was right next to them, working 60 to 70 hours a week, but it didn't even seem like working.

When you are the new kid on the team, the other guys like to play rookie tricks on you. One of the oldest was when you were at the track. They'd say, "Hey, go over to the 43 car and ask them if they've got a 'long weight.'"

So you'd go over and ask the Petty crew chief if he had a "long weight."

He'd say, "Hang on a minute while I check." He'd leave and be gone for a while. Then he'd come back and say he couldn't find it and that this or that other crew must have borrowed it and go check with them. So you'd go ask the next crew for a "long weight." And it would be the same thing. After the third or fourth crew, you'd catch on that a "long weight" was really a "long wait."

Or they'd send you out to borrow a "steel-braided hose stretcher." There is no such thing. There were guys who were really good at doing things like that. Barry Dodson and Dale Inman, when he was at Petty, were two of them. Doug Williams, who worked for Bud Moore for years, was really a master at that stuff. Things like that were kind of an initiation, I guess, into the world of big-time racing. You weren't just automatically accepted. You had to go through a kind of probation when you were proving to the other people on the team that you could cut it and that you belonged.

Of course, the person I really had to prove myself to was the boss—Junior Johnson.

I'd been introduced to Junior before I ever started working for him, but you couldn't say I "knew" him. And for the first month or so, he never called me by my name. It was always "Hey, boy."

Finally, I got a little worried, and I went to Herb Nab. I said, "Does Junior know who I am and what's going on?"

Herb said, "Don't you worry about a thing. I promise you Junior knows what's going on. He's just testing you."

Well, in those days, we didn't have airplanes like they do now, and we drove to all the races, and Junior went with us. He was very, very sensitive about the way people drove. If you didn't do it the way he liked it, he'd tell you about it. So one day, we were leaving the shop to go to a race, and he said to me, "Hey, boy, can you drive?"

"I think so, sir," I said.

"Well, don't be weaving all over the damned road," Junior said.

So I get behind the wheel, and I'm driving, and I'm pretty

intimidated, thinking that if I don't drive the way Junior likes, he's going to fire me—or chew me out anyway. But I drove all the way to Atlanta. When we got there, Junior looked over at Herb and said, "I think I found me a driver."

So for the next few years, I was the designated driver for Junior Johnson, a man many people considered to be the greatest driver who ever lived.

We worked hard in those days because we had to. We didn't have the money in racing that there is now. We didn't have backup cars, so we had to turn things around. If we crashed in a race on Sunday, we had to get the car back to the shop that evening, unload it, strip it, put the chassis back on the truck, and get it up to Banjo Mathews in Ashville, North Carolina, ready for his shop to straighten out first thing Monday morning. So you went flat out and sometimes you just couldn't stop for a while and sleep. The longest I ever went was 52 hours without going to bed.

But, you know, I never minded it because I loved what I was doing, and there was this great sense of teamwork. That's one of the things that I like most about racing—the feeling of belonging to a team and being part of something. You don't want to be the weak link, the one who lets Junior Johnson and Cale Yarborough down.

And it was fun. I remember Flossie—Junior's wife—would bring ham biscuits out to us when we needed something to eat. And when we weren't under the gun, we'd do things like help Junior plant the garden, milk the cows, slaughter hogs, and do other chores around the farm. Junior was always really strong on his coon dogs, and I'd go with him, some nights. Every now and then, we'd catch a coon alive and bring it back so we could put a collar on it and use it to train the dogs. You ever try putting a collar on a coon? I'm here to tell you it ain't easy.

Junior and Flossie didn't have any children, and they treated some of those dogs like they were their kids. I helped Junior bury some of those dogs. We made coffins for them out of wood or aluminum, depending on what we had around. Junior loved those dogs and wanted to give them proper funerals.

You could never be sure what Junior had in mind when he came in the shop looking for someone to help him with something. It was a good idea not to be standing around the Coke machine like you didn't have anything better to do. You might wind up like I did one day, fixing Junior's chicken manure spreader. There was a part broken inside of it, and I had to crawl up in there and weld it, breathing all that ammonia from the chicken litter. I believe it was the sickest I've ever been. I was about to throw up the whole time. At the end of the day, I couldn't take enough showers to get that smell off my skin and out of my hair.

Junior was around all the time, and he knew everything that was going on. And he had a way of letting you know how he wanted things done. It came out in the form of suggestions, or maybe casual observations, but you learned really quickly that it was best to pay attention to whatever it was he was "suggesting." Everyone had so much respect for Junior Johnson that it was like that old E.F. Hutton ad. When Junior spoke, you listened.

I guess I learned more about racing from Junior than I did from anybody—probably because Junior knew more about racing than anybody. He was a giant; first as a driver—with 50 wins and more than 90 top 3 finishes in the 313 races he started—and then as an owner—with 119 wins and 6 championships. Whichever hat Junior was wearing—driver or owner—he wore it better than anybody ever had.

Like I said earlier, I had actually been lucky enough to see Junior race, toward the end of his career, before I ever went to work for him. The first time was at a local, Charlotte dirt track on Sugar Creek

Road. It was a night race, and my dad took me there. Junior was running and so were Ned Jarrett and Cale Yarborough, which is kind of interesting when you consider that when I went to work for Junior, our driver was Cale.

A year after that race, I was sitting on the back straightaway at Charlotte Motor Speedway when Junior, Ned, and Fireball Roberts crashed. That was the race I mentioned earlier, where Fireball got burned so badly that he eventually died. A lot of people blamed Junior for that wreck, but it wasn't really anything he did. They were just racing hard. That was Junior's style. He was always a hard charger. But it got to Junior, I think, because Fireball was one of his best friends in racing. Not long after that, Junior retired from driving. He said he didn't feel like the challenge was there. It may have been that without Fireball on the track, Junior didn't feel like he had anyone to beat.

But it is for sure that in his prime, Junior was one of the greatest ever. The whole story of Junior Johnson, the driver, sounds like a legend. There was a famous magazine article written about him in the early '60s, by Tom Wolfe. It was called *Junior Johnson is the Last American Hero*, and I guess it was one of the first things to kind of put stock car racing and NASCAR on the map. Not many people outside of the South knew much about our kind of racing before then or took it very seriously if they did. They figured it for just a bunch of rednecks banging around little dirt tracks. We knew there was more to it than that, and, gradually, the rest of the country learned, too.

But about Junior . . . he was pretty much the perfect Southern stock car driver. He came from Wilkes County, North Carolina, and came by his driving style from running moonshine that his family made. Junior knew every road and every turn in every hollow in those hills, and he knew how to drive a car so nobody could catch him. Not any federal revenuer, for sure. This kind of driving is where the term "bootleg turn" comes from. You'd stand on the brakes, whip the wheel, do a 180, and be heading back the way you'd come, past the car that had been chasing you, going the other way. That kind of driving—and that move—was immortalized in the movie *Thunder Road* with Robert Mitchum.

Even though they never caught Junior hauling liquor, he did get arrested for making moonshine. At the shop, he told us the story. Seems Junior, his dad, and his brothers had been out late the night before, and it was Junior's turn to get up early and go up and stoke the fire so they could get the smoke down and have good coals for cooking the mash.

"You ever get the feeling . . . prickles running up the back of your neck, like someone is watching you? Well, I was standing there, stoking the fire, and I got that feeling," Junior said. "Out of the corner of my eye, I saw these fellows sneaking up on me. Well, I was holding a shovel, and I spun around and smacked one of them up the side of the head with that shovel. Then down through the woods I went with the rest of them in hot pursuit."

Well, back in those days, just because you saw somebody doing something illegal, that wasn't good enough. You had to catch him. Now Junior was a big guy, but he was moving fast, down through those woods, and he said they never would have caught him if he hadn't tripped and three of them jumped on top of him and held him down.

The way Junior told it, that was the end of the funny part. He was arrested and convicted. He went to prison and got what he called, "a rude education." There were some bad people in there, and one of the ways Junior made it was by getting with some other boys from Wilkes County who had already been sent up for doing liquor. They watched out for each other, but even so, Junior said he got in several fights in prison.

There were some people who thought that Junior got caught driving a car that was loaded with white lightning, but if you've ever had the "pleasure"—I guess you'd call it—of driving back through Wilkes County at night, coming from Bristol, Tennessee, on those mountain roads, you'll know that would have been just about impossible. It's an exciting experience; let me put it that way. It was never any secret that Junior Johnson could drive a car. He was as good on the back country roads as he was on a superspeedway. Maybe better.

But Junior wasn't the only good driver around. When he was racing, he was going against a lot of other men who could drive. What made Junior different was that he was always thinking, trying new things, and looking for that little edge. Junior wasn't just competitive and hard charging—even though that was a big part of what made him great—he was also *smart*. He might look and talk like a slow country boy, but Junior Johnson has a real sharp, real active mind.

When Junior retired from driving and became an owner, he kept looking for ways to win, to get that extra little something out of the car. He taught us to use every advantage, every little crease in the rules. If the rule book didn't say you *couldn't* do something, then you went ahead and did it. If you found out that it gave you an advantage, you kept right on doing it unless they rewrote the rule book and said you couldn't do it. Then you looked for something else.

For instance, if the rule book said you had to use a carburetor that weighed this much and measured that much, then you did it. But you looked around and if the book didn't say you couldn't change the boosters and you couldn't change the base plate, then you started fooling around with those things, looking for that edge. And when they made a rule that said you've got to run this particular base plate, then you figured since they didn't say you couldn't drill extra holes in the base plate you did that.

Of course, some people *did* cheat outright. Sometimes they got away with it, and sometimes they got caught. There is an old saying in NASCAR: "If you're going to cheat, then cheat neat." In fact, at Daytona the year I went to work for Junior, NASCAR came down hard on Darrell Waltrip and A.J. Foyt—along with some others—for using nitrous oxide when they were qualifying. You can get a really quick rpm boost with laughing gas, and guys were using it to qualify faster. NASCAR got suspicious and did some inspections, and those cars wound up having to requalify.

Foyt said he didn't know there was illegal fuel in his car.

"I just drive it," he said.

Waltrip, though, ran his mouth and probably said more than he should have. (He did this a lot, which was something I learned first-hand a few years later when he was Junior's driver and I was his crew chief.) At Daytona that year, Darrell said, "In NASCAR racing, there are a lot of things you have do to keep up with the competition. It's common knowledge that cheating in one form or another is part of it. If you don't cheat, you look like an idiot. If you do it and you don't get caught, you look like a hero. It you do it and get caught, you look like a dope. Put me in the category where I belong."

The rules about using laughing gas were as clear as they could be, and everyone knew them. Darrell and A.J. got caught. Simple as that. But there was a lot of gray in the rule book, and Junior's attitude was if you want to win, you study the rule book for what it *doesn't* say as much as for what it does.

So we weren't *necessarily* cheating, but we were always looking for some kind of advantage where the rules weren't really clear or, maybe, where there weren't any rules at all.

Of course, everybody else was doing the same thing. The trick was to do it better.

And then when you did come up with something, you wanted to keep it to yourself. When the other teams saw you were running faster or handling better, they wanted to find out what you were doing so they could copy it. But it wasn't easy to find out what another team was doing. There was more respect back then. Maybe more fear, too. If someone thought you were spying, he might come after you in the parking lot. In those days, we had some fights; that's how you settled things. It wasn't like today where you take somebody to court. Also, in those days, there wasn't so much movement of people from team to team. You could keep something a secret for a while. You had loyalty, and when you went to work for a team, you stayed there season after season. These days, you have people moving around all the time, getting a new deal from a different operation. The old team loyalty is gone.

When I think about it, that's probably one of the biggest changes in the sport since I've been involved. In my early days, NASCAR was really family oriented. The France family—Big Bill and then Bill Jr.—ran the sport. And you had really successful family racing operations like the Pettys from Level Cross, North Carolina, and the Allisons from Hueytown, Alabama. They didn't like each other, almost the way that the old clans feuded, not for any particular reason—none that anyone could remember anyway. If you were a Hatfield, then you didn't like McCoys. If you were Richard Petty, then you and Bobby Allison had a feud going, and when you were racing, you got after each other and mixed it up and swapped paint and all of that. It's the way things were.

Most of the old family operations have fallen behind these days. The Pettys and the Allisons both had promising, young, next-generation drivers killed. Adam Petty and Clifford and Davey Allison were going to carry the family fortunes, and when they were gone, the family operations lost something. But it happened with the other families, like the Woods, too. Back in my early days, the Wood brothers were winning 10 and 11 races a season, running a limited schedule, with David Pearson driving for them. Now they are having a hard time winning at all. And they have a good driver in Ricky Rudd.

The whole sport just got so much bigger, more sophisticated, and corporate. It's big, big business now. The old feuding family days are gone and won't be coming back. There are still France family people in charge, but NASCAR is listed on the New York Stock Exchange. That's how far things have come.

I don't think any of us saw how big it would get, back when I started working for Junior. In those days, we didn't think of it as business. We were more like cowboys in the old West, working for some particular outfit. We rode for the brand.

Junior Johnson was the patriarch, and we did things his way. We looked for every little advantage we could find to beat the other outfits. And because Junior was so good and so smart and wanted to win so badly, that's exactly the way it turned out when we had a good day. And for the first few years I was there, we had a lot of really good days.

*T*hings were starting to really take off for NASCAR when I hired on with Junior in mid-1976. It was, you might say, the start of the golden age. Good things were happening, finally, after several years when it seemed like if it hadn't been for bad news, there wouldn't have been any news for NASCAR at all.

The '70s started with factory sponsorship drying up. In the '60s,

there had been a feeling among the big three car manufacturers that racing was a good way to test product and, also, good for sales. "Win on Sunday, sell on Monday" was what everyone believed, and it seemed to work. When Richard Petty took a race in that blue Plymouth—and he won a bunch of them—you knew there would be a lot of Road Runners sold the next week. But, gradually, the people in the executive suites of the car manufacturers who believed in racing were replaced by bean counters who didn't.

In 1971, Ford's sponsorship was gone. Then Chrysler cut way back so only the Petty operation was getting support. This meant people like Bobby Isaac, Charlie Glotzbach, and Bobby Allison—all of them great drivers—didn't have rides.

When the big three got out of racing, a lot of talent left NASCAR. There just wasn't enough money around to keep some of the operations going. Cale Yarborough went to driving Indy cars. Junior Johnson and Banjo Mathews, who had been two of Ford's top team owners, got out when Ford quit racing. You had plenty of tracks and lots of events, but there weren't a lot of cars showing up for them. One short track event at Asheville had only 17 cars in the field, and only a couple of them had any chance of winning. Richard Petty blew everyone's doors off and won the race by 4 laps over Elmo Langley. That wasn't what the people came out and paid money to watch. So you had events where only 15,000 to 20,000 people would show up. That wasn't enough for the track owners and promoters to stay in business.

Then, as if NASCAR didn't have enough headaches with the factories pulling out of racing, here came the OPEC oil embargo. The government asked everyone to cut back on energy use by 25 percent. Gas stations were closing on the weekends.

But NASCAR had good leadership from Bill France, who came back from retirement and put together a plan to cut the length of races by 10 percent, reduce the amount of fuel that could be burned in practice, and make a few other changes that kept NASCAR in compliance and still running races.

There was some other good news, too. Junior Johnson had been talking to R.J. Reynolds in the early '70s about sponsoring a car. The big tobacco company was interested and, in fact, had bigger ideas than Junior. Cigarette advertising had been kicked off television, and the tobacco companies had a lot of marketing money to spend. NASCAR made a deal with RJR, and that was when the Grand National became the Winston Cup.

Another piece of good news came when Junior Johnson brought a Chevrolet team to the 600-mile race at Charlotte in 1971 with Charlie Glotzbach as his driver. It was a great time for Chevrolet to be coming back. There hadn't been factory support since 1963, no Chevy had been competitive since 1967, and Junior was still one of the most popular figures in racing. The man who put the deal together tried to talk Junior into driving the car, but he wouldn't do it. Even so, as a car builder, Junior was a draw, and the Chevy took the pole. They got a record crowd for the race: almost 80,000. Glotzbach crashed, but Junior was back in racing, running in selected events, and he won at Bristol later in the year. So that was good for racing.

The next year, Bobby Allison was driving for Junior in the Chevrolet. This led to even better things.

Still the early '70s were tough, and I think there were two things that held NASCAR together and kept it in shape for when the turnaround came: some great personalities and television.

NASCAR has always been about bigger-than-life drivers, and in the '70s you had some giants at their peaks. There was Richard Petty, of course. The King. He had that million-watt smile and a style of driving that just wouldn't let up. Petty knew only one way to go—flat on the floor. Then you had David Pearson, who hardly ever raced a full schedule and almost always won. He was one of the greatest technicians ever to sit behind a wheel. You had Buddy Baker and Benny Parsons. Bobby and Donnie Allison. They were all great drivers and had intensely loyal followings.

The competition between the drivers was fierce, and that was what really kept the fans interested. There is nothing in sports like a great rivalry, and NASCAR had them.

Probably the best rivalry in the early '70s, was Petty/Allison. Those two ran hard all the time, but especially against each other. There was just something there that brought out a little extra hunger in both of them. There was nobody on the track they wanted to beat more than each other.

In 1972, Allison was driving for Junior, and he and Petty really got into it. At Richmond, they were running away from everyone, and Petty tapped Allison and then got under him to take the lead. On the next lap, Allison got hard into Petty's bumper and put him up on top of the guardrail so it looked like he was going clean out of the track. But Petty held on, gathered it up, and got it back on the track. And he did it without losing the lead or the race. His fans just about went crazy.

Petty and Allison kept it up in the next couple of races, and at North Wilkesboro they got into it again on the last 3 laps. When Petty tried to pass on the high side, Allison put him into the guardrail. Allison's car was smoking from where the right side tires were rubbing up against the sheet metal, and it looked like he was on fire. Petty's car was a wreck. Parts from his car were lying all over the track. When Allison came around on the last lap, he had to run up the high side to miss all the debris, and Petty went under him to win the race. It was like that a lot with those two, and the fans just ate it up.

The thing that made it great for racing was that a lot of this was showing up on television. There is nothing for exposure in sports like getting your events on television, and in the '70s, that started happening for NASCAR. It wasn't necessarily live coverage, at first, and never flag to flag. But ABC's *Wide World of Sports* started showing the last parts of some races with highlights from the early laps. In the beginning, they got some dud races and missed some of the best stuff, especially a spectacular wreck by Petty. ABC had a malfunction with the replay equipment and missed the whole thing. After a couple of really bad races, with only a few cars finishing and none of them on the same lap, ABC started running the footage a few weeks after the race, using it to fill airtime between other events. Still it was a start, and the people at ABC—especially Roone Arledge—seemed to understand that racing had a strong fan base and would make great television someday.

So ABC hung in there, and eventually they started to get some good racing on television. They got a real break in 1976 at Daytona. This was early in the season, before I started working for Junior, so I wasn't at the track when it happened. Like a lot of people, I saw it at home on television.

ABC was broadcasting the last half of the race—they still didn't have flag-to-flag coverage—and with a little more than 20 laps to go, it had come down to Petty and David Pearson. Pearson was barely hanging on to the lead until Petty passed him with 13 to go. For the next 12, it was a real nail-biter. They were nose to tail, and then Pearson went high and Petty ducked under to slingshot him for the finish. They got into it, door to door. Pearson caught the wall, and when he spun, that spun Richard. They went down into the infield, and both cars looked like they belonged in the junkyard instead of on the track. Richard was about 100 feet from the finish line, and he couldn't re-fire his engine. Pearson managed to limp across the finish at about 20 mph, so he got the checkered flag. But NASCAR was the big winner. It was a great finish, and you had to love it even if you didn't know anything about racing.

Not long after that, CBS negotiated with NASCAR for the rights to broadcast the 1979 Daytona 500—live and flag to flag. It turned out to be another great race and an even wilder finish. I was there for that one, in the pits, and my driver was involved, so we'll get to that later.

So after a really shaky start, the decade was ending with lots of good news for racing. Television was coming in big. Winston was aboard. People were finding sponsors for their teams, and great drivers were running great races. It was my good luck to be getting in at just the right time with a great owner and a great driver.

I haven't said too much, up till now, about our driver. Truth is, though, Cale Yarborough was one of the greatest drivers in the history of stock car racing and a personal hero of mine. He was a real man's man—not physically big like Junior—but tough as they come. Cale was capable and confident, and he did a lot of things, all of them well. Cale was a farmer and an outdoorsman, a pilot and a sky diver, and he could drive a race car with the best of them. He was good-natured and naturally friendly in a country sort of way, but you surely didn't want to cross him because he would fight you.

Cale wasn't much of a presence around the shop during the week when we were working on the car. This was a different time, and a lot of the drivers weren't really that involved in what went on around the shop. Cale would fly into wherever we were racing for practice and qualifying, and then he'd run the race and fly home until the next week. We'd take the car back to Ronda and work on it and meet him late that week at whatever track we were running. That was pretty much the way things were in racing back then.

Still, Cale and I got to be pretty close. We'd go out and do things together, especially when we were at Darlington for the Labor Day race. We'd finish qualifying on Saturday, and we'd have Sunday off before the race. So we'd go out to Cale's farm, which was close by, and shoot dove. Cale was a great shot. He was also a great storyteller and could tell jokes that would just break you up. Cale purely enjoyed life, and his enthusiasm and good humor were contagious.

I didn't think there was a driver in the world who could give any more than Cale Yarborough did. He had more heart than any man I've ever seen drive a race car. Cale wasn't very technical about helping us get the car set up, but once he got under that wheel, whatever the car lacked, he figured a way to drive it so he was in the race. Cale would tell us, "Boys, just get it close; I'll make up the difference."

And when Cale pulled those gloves up, you just couldn't believe what he could do with a race car. He'd drive the wheels off of it. I saw that in my first race with the team in early September at Richmond. Cale and Richard Petty were locked in a close points race for the Winston Cup, with Cale just a little ahead when the race started. From here on, it wasn't just every race that counted. Every *lap* counted. You didn't want to be the one to screw it up when you were the new kid on a team where Junior Johnson was your owner, Cale Yarborough was your driver, and you were running nose to nose with Richard Petty for the championship.

You can imagine how I felt, going up to Richmond for my first race as part of the team for the 11 car. I wasn't just going into the big time; I was going to the very top of the big time. It wasn't just about racing. I already knew about racing. And it wasn't just about winning. That's what you are in racing to do—win. But this was being with the people who I'd looked up to for what seemed like all my life and racing against someone who a lot of people considered the greatest driver of them all and a man who had been my favorite ever since my first hero, Fireball Roberts, had wrecked at Charlotte and later died. It seemed almost unbelievable, but it was true. I was in the pits there at Richmond, where my driver was running against Petty. Even though I wasn't working over the wall, changing tires or refueling, I was still part of the team, and people were depending on me. I needed to make sure that I put things in the right places and that when somebody needed something, I could put my hands on it and get it to him. I had my job, and if I didn't do it right, the team would suffer. So I was feeling the pressure.

We won that first race. Cale had Bobby Allison trying to chase him down and right on his bumper when he took the flag. Petty was third. We were still leading for the Cup by 44 points. And there I was, on Victory Lane after my first race. It was like Disney World, baby. Nothing could have been sweeter.

But, you know, in racing you don't spend a lot of time celebrating your last race because you've got to be ready to qualify for another race in less than a week. So we did a little backslapping, told each other "good job," and then we started loading everything up—all the tires and the tools and the car. Then we got on the road and headed back to the garage in Ronda to get ready for that next race.

This was something new to me and something I had to get used to really quickly. NASCAR was always about the next race. You were always looking ahead, and you never had any time to waste. A few years after that first win in Richmond, I was at Daytona—I had worked my way up to crew chief by then—and my driver had just won the biggest race of all. And you know what I did as soon as we were finished celebrating on Victory Lane and getting our pictures taken for the papers? I put everybody to work loading the truck, and then I got on the road and drove straight back to Charlotte, nonstop. That's more than 500 miles. I was so pumped that I never really thought about going to sleep. I knew I had to start getting ready Monday morning for the next race, and I was eager to get going. I liked winning and wanted more. But I'm pretty sure I would have felt the same way if we'd lost. I would have hated losing so much that I would have been chomping at the bit, wanting to get at the car and do whatever it took to start winning. In NASCAR, you're never sitting still or even going slow.

So after that first win, it was back to working on the car. In those first weeks with the team, I was doing whatever they told me to do. I was sweeping floors, welding, pulling dents, finding tools, and, for some reason, they had me working a lot changing spark plugs. We worked 8 hours, at least, every day and sometimes 14. But I didn't really notice because I was so glad to be where I was and because we were winning.

We won at Dover, the week after Richmond. Cale got black-flagged for running over a jack in pit lane, but he made that lap up and was running on the lead lap when he had ignition troubles and went down 2 laps to Petty and David Pearson. Things looked pretty bad for our chances right then, but I noticed that Junior didn't really seem all that concerned. He just stood there with his foot up on a tire, looking out at turn four watching the action. That's the picture of Junior that comes to my mind when I think about him at the track. He seldom looked either excited or discouraged. He looked like a man who was studying the action and taking it all in. That's the way he approached just about everything, whether it was at the track or back in the garage. Junior didn't let his emotions get on top of him or get in the way of his thinking.

Cale kept fighting back at Dover, got back on the lead lap, and started closing in on Petty. He passed him with 21 laps to go and won the race. It was just plain gutsy, determined driving, and it made us all feel proud. We left Dover up 54 points on Petty.

And that was big, leading in the points race, but maybe not as big as it is now. You wanted to win the Cup, of course, but it wasn't as important back then as it is now. What you wanted to do, more than anything, was win *races*. And some races were more important than others. Daytona was the biggest, for sure. Then you wanted to win at Darlington, Charlotte, and Talladega. Those were the big four, the grand slam of stock car racing. They were all run on superspeedways—long, high-banked tracks—where the crowds were bigger and so was the money.

Winning the championship has gotten to be a bigger and bigger thing until more and more teams these days build a racing strategy around it. The reason for this is exposure. If you win the Cup, it puts you in a great negotiating position. You've got your sponsorship and promotional deals sewed up. And that's one of the biggest challenges in racing—finding the money.

There are a couple of races where winning can do almost as much for you as taking the Cup. That's especially true of Daytona. Michael Waltrip has only won two races; but since both of them have been the biggest race of all, the Daytona 500, he is a very bankable driver.

Back when we started, the individual wins were more important. They kept your name in the papers, and they won you money. And, no doubt, it's a lot more fun to win a race than it is just to finish high and bank a few points that will keep you competitive in the standings. Racing is about being out front. And in my first two races, that's where we'd finished.

And we kept right on going the next 2 weeks. We won at Martinsville, and we won at North Wilkesboro. That one was sweet because the governor of North Carolina was there to declare "Cale Yarborough Day." Cale did the right thing by winning the race. Petty came in third and dropped a little further back in the points race, and we were looking good for the championship. I might have been thinking that we'd never lose, but I doubt it. I was young, but I'd been around racing long enough to know better than that.

Sure enough, we ran second in the next one, at Charlotte, but it wasn't official until a couple of hours after the race. Even after NASCAR did a really careful tear-down inspection of Donnie Allison's engine, Herb Nab was still sure that it wasn't legal. Herb wanted an independent inspection to see if Allison was running a big engine, but he didn't get it. Petty ran eighth and then won the next race, at Rockingham. But Cale ran fifth, so we were still up by almost 100 points, with only two races to go, and looking solid for the championship. Petty wasn't quitting though. He told the press, "Two races ain't enough time for me to win, but it is enough time for him to lose."

We didn't intend to lose, though. We made really sure before that next race, at Atlanta, that the car was ready and that we'd run good and finish the race. We didn't want to go out because of a blown engine or a dropped transmission or because we'd overlooked something or done something stupid. You wouldn't believe how much I fussed over those spark plugs that week.

And it turned out that it was Petty who couldn't finish. We ran good, and Cale took fourth and might have done better if we hadn't had a flat tire close to the finish. So that just about sewed it up. All we had to do was start the next race, at Ontario, California, and the Cup was ours. What I remember most about that Atlanta race was Dale Earnhardt wrecking a car. Dale and I were friends in those days, and like a lot of people, I was pulling for him to make it in Cup racing, but he was having his troubles. I'd seen him run his first Cup race, at Charlotte, back in '76. I was crewing for Walter Ballard—it was a couple of months before I went to work full-time, for Junior—

and Dale was driving. Before he ran a full lap, he wrecked the car—dropped the transmission.

Walter was so mad he told Dale, "Son, you ought to quit right now because you couldn't drive nails even if somebody gave you a hammer."

Dale, of course, didn't have any quit in him. Not in that race, which he managed to get back into and finish once we got the transmission working, or in any other. But he struggled a long time before he succeeded. That race at Atlanta where we sewed up the points race was just his third Cup start. He was driving a Chevrolet for Johnny Ray—not a great ride, but Dale was taking what he could get back then—when a driver named Dick Brooks caught the wall on the third turn and bounced out right in front of Dale.

Dale hit Brooks and started going end over end, down the track, with the car flying apart every time it flipped. You see a lot of crashes in NASCAR racing, and you don't ever really get to the point where one doesn't at least make you think. But this one was one of the scariest and most spectacular wrecks I'd ever seen, and I was worried for Dale. Most of his car was just debris on the track. They took Dale to the track hospital and looked him over. He was okay, and everyone was relieved when they released him.

Funny, there was another Chevrolet in that race that did not finish. That one was driven by Richard Childress, who was also having a tough year. He finished 11th in the total points. Later on, the two of them would team up—Childress as owner and Earnhardt driving—and dominate NASCAR.

But that was still a few years off in the future. The 1976 season ended at Ontario with Cale Yarborough 195 points ahead of Richard Petty. We were NASCAR champions. The official awards ceremony would come in a couple of months, at Daytona, during Speedweeks. Meanwhile, we had to get the car back across the country, to North Carolina, in time to have Thanksgiving with our families. Then we would start getting ready for the next season.

I couldn't wait.

*T*he off-season was short but sweet. I got to spend Thanksgiving

with family and friends. Christmas, too. And it was nice to come home

a winner. My dad was proud of me, and I was grateful to him for the

advice he'd given me about holding out until I got the right deal. I'd

listened to him, I'd waited, and I was with the team that had just won

the Winston Cup. That seemed like the right deal to both of us.

I was looking forward to my first full season with Junior Johnson,

Cale Yarborough, and the rest of the team. If we'd won it in '76, there

wasn't any reason we couldn't go back out and win it again in '77.

But winning doesn't get to be a habit just because you want it to be.

You have to work at it.

Winning was a good enough reason for me to want the new season

to start, but it wasn't the only one. I had my own goals, too. One of

them was to learn as much as I could from Junior, Herb Nab, and the other guys so I could start working my way up and taking on more responsibility. I wasn't always going to be the new kid, and one day, I wanted to be the boss. Not an owner, necessarily. But I could see myself as a crew chief one day. I was young, and I didn't even have a full season with Junior under my belt, but I had ambition. However, I had enough sense to know I still had a lot to learn.

The new season started where the last one had ended—in California. We went out to Riverside and ran good, but we finished second when Cale spun with just a few laps to go and David Pearson got in front of him and won the race. It was disappointing, but we still left California tied with Pearson for first in Cup points. The system rewards you for things besides winning the race, including leading laps and finishing. We had a good car, a great driver, and a really solid chance in the biggest race of all—Daytona.

I guess every sport has its signature event. In baseball, you've got the World Series, and in football, there's the Super Bowl. NASCAR has the Daytona 500 and Speedweeks. The Daytona 500 is a tradition going back to when NASCAR started in the '40s. Back then, they actually ran a part of the race on the beach. That's just a memory now, along with crowds in the low thousands. Daytona has grown from those modest beginnings into Speedweeks: a huge 2-week celebration that is sort of a stock car Mardi Gras. Every racing fan wants to go to Daytona, and about a quarter of a million of them show up for the race that every team wants to win. It's the big one.

This year, Daytona was even more special than usual for our team because we were the winners of the '76 Winston Cup, and the awards banquet was held in Daytona. We met in a banquet room in a local hotel, dressed in our usual clothes. We ate tough roast beef and listened to a lot of speeches. The crew chiefs got trophy belt buckles, and the rest of us got jackets with decals that showed we were Winston Cup champs. It seemed like a really big deal at the time—

certainly to a kid who was just in his first full season—and I don't think any of us had any idea at the time that in a few years we'd all be going up to New York and wearing tuxedos to the awards dinner at the Waldorf-Astoria hotel. We all knew that NASCAR was big and getting bigger. But none of us could have imagined how big it would get.

For me, Daytona was plenty big enough. I'd been there before, and I'd crewed there before but never for a champion and a real contender in the biggest race of all. I was feeling more confident about myself and my importance to the team, even though I was still working mostly on the other side of the wall. I changed tires some in those first couple of seasons, but it wasn't really a good idea for me to be out there doing that because my knee locked up on me sometimes. I'd torn some cartilage playing football in high school and college, and a chip would float up into the wrong place from time to time. It happened to me once in a race, and we didn't want it to happen again. Especially not at Daytona.

But I was there, doing my part, especially in the garage. And on race day, it paid off. Cale ran hard and held off Benny Parsons. After Cale took the checkered flat, the whole crew climbed on top of the Chevrolet for a ride to victory lane. That was sweet.

So we left Daytona as double winners. They gave us the Cup at the awards banquet, and then we went out and won the biggest race on the NASCAR calendar. I was living a dream.

With two races down, we had a first and a second. In the points, we were looking in our mirror at a driver who'd won only four races in his career, compared to Cale's 41. But that driver was somebody you didn't want to underestimate and couldn't ignore. He wouldn't let you because he had probably the biggest mouth in all of racing. His name is Darrell Waltrip. He and Cale ran close all year, and their rivalry was as good as any in the history of racing. And, of course, Waltrip and I went on to have our own history, but that story comes later.

Cale won five of the first nine races that year. Richard Petty won two, and Waltrip won at Darlington. It was the first time Waltrip had ever won a race on one of the big tracks, and he was saying that it was proof he had "arrived." He ran a good race—no denying it—but one win at Darlington wasn't the same as one at Daytona and four others. We also had that second out in California and a third at Atlanta.

The fact was, the car was running great, and we were winning most of our races and finishing all of them. That was a real credit to Junior and the team. Nothing hurts like those DNFs—Did Not Finish— when either the driver got in a bad wreck or the equipment failed. One thing I learned really quickly—and saw every week—was that Junior Johnson ran a money-making operation. There is a saying you hear a lot around the track, "You can make a small fortune in racing. But you've got to have a large fortune when you start out."

Junior didn't think that way. He wanted to win as much as anyone, naturally, but he was in racing to make money. He knew you weren't going to win them all. But if you couldn't win, then you wanted to get a top five. And if you couldn't get a top five, then finish in the top ten. And if that wasn't possible, then make sure that you at least finished the race. You wanted to get your lap money and your points. And, if you started a race with a car that maybe wasn't the fastest but was mechanically as good as you could make it, then you might just outlast the faster cars and sneak across the finish line ahead of them if they had problems late in the race.

A lot of races have been won by slower cars that hung in there and finished when a $5 part broke down on the faster car. I've seen it— more than once. And it has happened to me—more than once.

This was just one more thing I learned from Junior. You make the car as good as you can, and even if you don't always win, good things will happen.

Actually, that's the way it worked out for Waltrip in the 10th race that season, at Talladega. It was a tough race—fast the way it always

is down there—with 63 different lead changes and four cars running close when it got down to the finish. Waltrip was leading with Cale, Benny Parsons, and Donnie Allison running close behind in the draft. Cale looked like he was set up to pass on the last lap, but he didn't quite make the move he had to, up on the high side, and Waltrip beat him by less than a third of a second. Cale wasn't happy about it and said something about how Waltrip had been lucky to win because of all the cars on the track, he'd been running the fourth fastest.

You didn't give Waltrip that kind of opportunity to get into it with his mouth.

"Well," Waltrip said, "I guess that it was just a case of superior driving."

Waltrip's team had been going through a little turmoil with some personnel changes. They'd brought in Derel Dierenger, a former driver who'd had a lot of success, to be something called "coordinator." Waltrip started complaining about how he didn't need a "babysitter." But they won right away at Darlington and then again at Talladega. Those were two big races, and that kind of quieted Waltrip down a little. But the crew chief, David Ifft, left because he couldn't get along with Dierenger, who wound up getting fired a couple of months later when they couldn't win another race.

All that was interesting to watch and read about, but we couldn't let ourselves feel too superior because we started having our own problems in the middle of the season. We were falling off—still finishing but not winning—and after leading all year in the points, all of a sudden we were looking up at Petty, who'd caught us at Pocono. Everybody was feeling frustrated, especially Cale. He ran second in the next race, at Talladega, but he wasn't happy with the car. He told the newspaper reporters that he had "the sorriest Chevrolet in racing" and that if he'd won the race he would have "been in court on Monday for stealing."

Junior, naturally, heard about that. Normally, Junior didn't do a lot of talking to the press, and he sure didn't talk down his driver or his team. But he had to make sure everyone knew who was in charge.

"We're in the middle of some engine problems right now," Junior said in an interview. "We're also in the middle of a championship battle. If Cale starts running his mouth, he'll be looking for another car. We don't have to listen to a bunch of lip from him."

It was another example of something I've talked about before—when Junior talked, you listened. Cale wasn't the only one on the team who was frustrated. We all were. But Junior understood that you don't fix things by running down the team or the car in public. You work things out together, or they don't get worked out. And if you can't be part of the team, then you need to hit the door. Junior never wanted anyone on the team who didn't want to be there.

So we went back to Ronda, and we went back to work. Two weeks later, we were back on Victory Lane at Bristol. At that race, we were fined when they found an illegal extra fuel tank in the car in the pre-race inspection. Junior said he was really surprised and didn't know *how in the world* that fuel tank got there. I don't think the NASCAR officials believed him. I don't think anyone in the whole world believed him.

So we had a little momentum going into September and the Southern 500 at Darlington on Labor Day. This is one of the great, traditional races run on the one of the classic NASCAR tracks. Every fan loves this race and knows the story of how in the late '40s, Harold Brasington built the mile-and-a-quarter track just off highway 151, out in the middle of nowhere, and how he had to make it pear shaped so he wouldn't disturb a minnow pond near turn two. The owner of the land, Mr. Ramsey, was particular about that minnow pond.

The Darlington track was probably the original "if you build it, they will come" sporting facility. When they ran the first Southern 500 there in 1950, more than 25,000 people turned out. That was huge, back then. The track at Darlington and that Labor Day race had a lot

Cale ran a great race on a hot day, and he beat Benny Parsons by less than a second. When Cale was interviewed after the race, he said it was one of the hardest races that he'd ever run, so physically punishing that he considered it dangerous.

Waltrip read the quote, and when he won the next race, at North Wilkesboro, he told reporters that he thought the race had been about "a one and a half on the Cale Scale" and went on to say something about how maybe our driver was getting to be "too old for this sport." At the time, Darrell was 30 and Cale was 38.

We didn't like anyone beating our driver or running our driver down, and we especially didn't like anyone talking about our driver *and* beating him. Petty was second to us in the points race, but he didn't have much of a chance of catching us. So right then, there wasn't anybody we wanted to beat more than Waltrip. I guess we thought we could shut him up if we beat him. But, like everybody else, we found out that nothing would shut Waltrip up. Nothing in the world.

Waltrip hurt his shoulder in practice a week or so later. Then before the race at Rockingham, he was riding a mule in a celebrity race and got thrown to the ground and stepped on by the mule. After the race, he was complaining about how bad he was hurting and talking about how he was about to "give out."

Cale heard it and said he felt fine and wished they added another 500 miles to the race. "Looks like Jaws is getting to old for this sport."

That was the last race we won that season. Waltrip took one more, in Atlanta, and naturally had something to say about how he'd "snatched victory from the jaws of defeat."

But at the end of the season, we'd won our second straight Winston Cup. It was pretty impressive winning two in a row. That doesn't happen very often, and we had a right to be proud. But I think we might have been prouder—the guys in the pits and the garage, anyway—of the way we'd won it. We started 30 races, and we fin-

ished 30 races. Nobody had finished every race he'd started since 1962 when a guy named Herman Beam did it.

It's kind of funny, but when Junior was a driver, he had a reputation for driving cars into the ground. A lot of the time, if Junior didn't win, he didn't finish because he'd blown the engine trying. He told people that his driving philosophy was really simple—"go or blow." But it was a different Junior Johnson when he was an owner and the goal was to make money. He set high standards. He wanted the car to be as mechanically right as it could possibly be, to give the driver every chance to finish the race and win if he could. To the guys who worked on the car, it felt like we had lived up to those expectations, and that was something to be proud of.

We had 9 wins, 25 top fives, and 27 top tens. You have to look hard to find a better record—and such a high level of consistency—anywhere in NASCAR history. That record gave us the feeling of being professionals at the absolute top of our game.

Cale won the "Olsonite Driver of the Year" award. Ten journalists who wrote about motor sports voted for it, and Cale was the third of Junior's drivers to win. The first two were LeeRoy Yarbrough—who was not related to Cale, even though a lot of people thought so, even though they spelled their names differently—and a driver who became one of our strongest, most bitter rivals, Bobby Allison.

In NASCAR, even a good season is a long season, and the team had been through a lot. I was still young and still learning. I'd seen how Junior handled things when we were falling off in the middle of the season, and I'd learned how it pays off to make sure of the little things that keep you in a race and get you to the finish line even when, for some reason, you don't win.

Junior had a really intuitive way of knowing when to push us and when to back off. Sometimes we just needed to take a break, and he seemed to know when that time was. I remember how once, when we

were getting ready for a race, he came through the shop and gathered everyone up and said, "Come on, boys, we're going fishing."

What he didn't bother to tell us was that his idea of fishing was "telephoning." That's where you take an old, hand-cranked telephone and run the wires off it down into a likely looking spot. You turn that crank and throw some electricity into the water. It stuns the fish, they just float up to the surface, and you grab them. Next to dynamite, it is about the most sure-fire way there is of catching catfish. And just as illegal.

Well, anyway, Junior pulled us all out of the shop, and we got some inner tubes. Then on the way to the river, Junior made another stop and picked up some refreshments—several jars of Wilkes County's finest, the same kind of stuff he hauled over the back roads and went to prison for making. It went by different names—Cherry Bounce is one—but it was all white lightning. Moonshine.

We all started floating down the Yatkin River, and we found a likely looking spot. We threw the wires in and cranked up some fish. We'd net 'em and put 'em in a burlap sack and then go on down to the next place and take a little drink from one of those jars on the way down.

After a while I said to Junior, "Hey, boss man, looks like you ain't drinking much of this good stuff."

He said, "No. Don't want to get too drunk."

"Afraid of drowning?"

"Naw," he said. "If the game warden comes along, he's going to catch the drunk ones, and I'm going to get away."

One thing about Junior Johnson—he always had a plan.

We must have caught 50 or 60 pounds of catfish. We went back to the shop and skinned them and had us a big fish fry. That was Junior's way of keeping us from getting too tight, even though we were running for championships.

to do with making NASCAR a success. It was still one of the biggest races on our calendar. People called Darlington, "the track too tough to tame," mostly because of how tight the turns were and how low they were banked. A lot of guys would hit the wall coming out of turn two to get the cars lined up going into the straight. This left a mark on the right quarter panel that was called "the Darlington stripe."

We liked it that we were going down to one of the big races leading in the points. We knew we had a good car and a great driver. Because the race wasn't until Monday, we had some time on the weekend. Cale took some of us out to his farm for a dove shoot. He was from South Carolina, and Darlington was almost his home track.

Come race day, Waltrip was ready, and so were we. The race was back and forth until one of the late laps. Waltrip got impatient and got into the back of a car that was driven by a guy named D.K. Ulrich. He got into Cale, and we had a four-car tangle that cost all of us some laps. We were all pretty mad at Waltrip because felt like we could have won it if it hadn't been for that crash. We got the car back on the track, and Cale drove it as hard as he could to take fifth.

After the race, Ulrich got in Cale's face. "How come you hit me?" he asked.

"Wasn't me who hit you," Cale said. "It was Jaws."

"Who?"

"Jaws. You know, Waltrip."

It was the first time anyone had called Waltrip that, but the name fit. Darrell was always jacking his jaws. Some people said he only stopped moving his mouth to change feet. Darrell admitted that the wreck was his fault, and the name stuck.

We kept running good in the next two races—took a fourth and a third—and toward the end of September when we went to Martinsville, things were looking good for a second straight Winston Cup. But that didn't shut Waltrip up.

After that first full year with Junior, I felt like I'd had 10 years worth of education in a year and a half of racing, but I knew I still had a lot to learn.

So I was ready, as soon as we got home from California, to get back to work and back to racing.

he team was even busier than usual during the off-season. The technology was changing, and a lot of it was because of the OPEC oil embargoes. Cars were getting smaller, and manufacturers were doing more to make them lighter and more fuel efficient. NASCAR was still a "stock car" racing outfit, which meant that the cars that were being raced were just like the cars down at the showrooms

and out on the highways. This was always more theoretical than real, and every year, the gap between the cars you saw on the track on Sunday and the ones you could buy on Monday was getting wider and wider.

With the new equipment that was coming in, Junior Johnson had to make some decisions. There are a lot of variables that go into making a race car go fast. One of them, obviously, is power. We all knew about that, and everyone spent a lot of time working on engines to get every last fraction of horsepower we could from a block that met the NASCAR specifications. You could still make a tweak here and a fix there—legal, of course—and get a slight advantage. But it was getting harder and harder.

And everyone was learning more and more about the "setup" on a car. You hear a lot about this from the announcers when you are watching a race and from the crew chiefs when they are interviewed. They'll say the car is "loose," or "tight," depending on how it handles, and they'll make changes by softening tires or putting more air in them, by fiddling with the shocks, or by putting wedges in the springs. Before a race, you can adjust the camber on the tires, according to the track you are running, so you'll get a firmer footprint. A lot of what goes on in the pits during a race, and in the garage between races, has to do with getting the setup right.

Junior Johnson and Banjo Mathews had been ahead of everyone on working with chassis setups to run faster and longer and win races. It was another case of Junior outthinking everybody else, and it had paid off for him over the years. But everybody had caught up or was getting close by the end of the '70s, and as with engines, you were talking about very small margins now.

That left aerodynamics. And that's where Junior was looking when we got ready to start the '78 season.

All sorts of things happen when you move a car faster and faster through the air, which is sitting out there in front of the hood like a big invisible wall. The car has to bore a hole through the air, and then the air flows around and over the car. Those forces do different things to the car. How the car performs in air—and how the air performs on the car—can have a lot to do with how well the car handles and how fast it goes.

When he was driving, Junior Johnson was first to discover what everyone calls "the draft." He was at Daytona one year, driving a car that was a long way from being the fastest on the track. He was telling his crew chief, Ray Fox, that his Chevrolet was at least 30 miles an hour slower than the guys in the Pontiacs. That might have been an exaggeration but not by much. Everyone in the Pontiacs was faster than Junior, especially Fireball Roberts.

Junior was out at practice one day, and the Pontiacs were blasting by him. On one lap, he tucked in behind Fireball, and *whoa hoss* it was like he got a 10 percent horsepower boost from a supercharger or something. Junior ran the fastest lap—by a lot—that he had run in practice, and he actually kept up with the Pontiac, staying right on its bumper.

Junior came into the pits, and Fox asked him, "What did you do to the car?"

"I didn't do anything," Junior said.

"Well, you must have done something. You ran the fastest lap you've ever run in that car. You were 10 miles an hour faster than you've ever been."

"I know," Junior said. "But I don't know *why*."

But Junior kept trying the same thing—ducking in behind one of the faster Pontiacs when it came by—and it kept happening. And gradually, he figured it out. The Pontiac in front of him had been opening a hole in the air, and if he got in close enough, he was carried along in the vacuum and pushed ahead by the air trying to fill up the hole. That's the simple explanation, anyway.

The important thing to Junior wasn't the precise science of aerodynamics—although I'm pretty sure he understood it well enough. He knew that by using what he called "the draft," he could get extra speed for no extra throttle and let the lead car do the heavy lifting of blasting a hole in the air. Junior won at Daytona in 1960 in a slower car because he was using the draft and nobody else understood it—or even really knew about it—yet. Junior was just that much ahead of everybody.

Or course, everybody else caught on really quickly, and pretty soon you couldn't win at the big tracks like Daytona unless you knew about the draft and how to work it. But even when it wasn't a secret anymore there were some drivers who just understood it better, and could play it better, than anyone else and for that reason always seemed to do better on the big tracks. The best example of this is probably Dale Earnhardt. He was the absolute master of the draft. People in racing used to say, "Earnhardt can *see* air." He was that good at working the draft. Funny thing is, so is Dale Jr. Maybe it's in the genes.

Even though the draft—and aerodynamics in general—was no secret anymore by the time I came along, Junior was still thinking about what air did to a car. And he was really interested in what the shape of the car would do to the air. This is why he was looking at Oldsmobiles and thinking about a change before the '78 season got started.

Now at that time, we were running the Chevy Laguna, which was basically Chevrolet's superspeedway car. We also had a Chevy Monte Carlo that had a similar roofline to the Oldsmobile that Junior was looking at because he liked the shape of the nose. It was more streamlined and might cut through the air better. So we mocked up the nose of the Olds, mounted it on the Monte Carlo, and took it down to Talladega to do some testing on the track. We called it our "Hillbilly Wind Tunnel."

Sure enough, the Chevy ran better with the Olds nose mounted on it than the Pontiac and Buick that we tried. So we made the change. Junior had been running Chevies for a while now, so this came as a shock to a lot of people, but not to the crew and not to people who'd been following racing for a long time. In Junior's early career, as a driver, he was always driving different kinds of cars, looking for the best combination of engine and chassis—power and handling—to get him to Victory Lane. Aerodynamics was just one more element.

Because everyone was catching on to the aerodynamic advantage, later in the '78 season, NASCAR had to start dealing with spoiler issues. The spoiler, you know, is that sort of wing on the rear end of the car. When the air flows over the spoiler, it forces the rear end of the car down so that you get a better tire grip and the car kind of sticks to the track. The more air, the more downforce. So you can run faster and faster.

But at the same time we were running faster and faster and getting up around the 200 mph mark—not just in NASCAR but in all kinds of racing, including Indy and Formula One—the cars were getting lighter and lighter. With lighter, faster cars, it gets harder and harder to make them stick to the track. They just want to take off, so the downforce that is created by the spoiler keeps the car from getting loose. Eventually, a combination of things, including aerodynamics and tire design, made it possible to run the big tracks so fast that NASCAR had to do something to slow the cars down. That's when they came up with restrictor plates.

But that's another discussion, for later on. Back to '78.

The change in cars wasn't the only thing going on. In the off-season, Herb Nab, who was our crew chief and the man who had hired me, told Junior that he was leaving to go with the Harry Ranier operation, where Lennie Pond was driving. That scared the heck out of me because we'd be getting a new crew chief. You never know, in that kind of situation, if the new man might want to clean house and bring in his own people.

Junior actually brought in two people—Tim Brewer and Travis Carter—to be co-crew chiefs. So now we had a new car and *two* new crew chiefs. What hadn't changed was the leadership—Junior was still our owner—and the driver. Cale Yarborough was back with us and wanting to get after it. He'd won two Cups in a row, and he wanted to make it three. No driver had ever done that, and Cale wanted to be the first. The rest of us wanted it as badly as he did.

And we started out on the right foot, winning on the road course at Riverside in California. Even though we couldn't quite get it done at Daytona, we still managed a second place finish after we had some equipment problems that cost us a lot more than the time we lost the race by, which was only 33 seconds. What we learned at Daytona was that we had a car that would compete on the superspeedways. So the Hillbilly Wind Tunnel stuff we'd done in the off-season was paying off. Once again, Junior Johnson had made the right decision.

But it wasn't an easy season. Any NASCAR season is tough on a team. The pace grinds you down even if nothing else does, and there is always something else. In our case, we knew we had the car, and the driver and the new co-crew chief arrangement seemed to be working out, so we had the team. So what was the problem?

Well, in any sport, getting to the top is very hard. But what is almost as hard as getting there is staying there. That's why the word "dynasty" carries so much weight when people talk about sports— any sport, from basketball to hockey to stock car racing. There are a lot of teams that have a great season, win a championship, but then can't defend it. They put it all together that one time, but when the next season comes, some of the parts are missing. People who'd gotten it done the year before are gone. Or maybe they just aren't as hungry as they were; they've gotten a little rich and a little complacent, and the competition wants it a little more than they do. It happens all the time.

And, of course, sometimes a team will ride a lucky streak to the championship. In racing, somebody will start a season with such a big advantage in equipment that by the time everybody else catches up— or NASCAR changes the rules—it's too late. You used to see that more in the old days than you do now, but it still happens.

Luck might win it for you once, but luck tends to even out over two or three seasons. We knew that we weren't just lucky; we were good.

We felt—and I think rightly so—that we were the best. We'd not only won two straight championships, in 1976 and 1977, we'd also put together one of the finest season-long performances in the history of the sport. Finishing every race in 1977 was something special, and it was a streak we were all proud of. It was like the defensive unit on a football team that hasn't let an opponent score a touchdown for several games. It gets to be really important to you, a way you have of measuring yourself, of proving just how good you are. And after a while, that record actually starts weighing on you, and you start to put pressure on yourself to hold on to it.

Three races into the season, we still had our streak going. We had a first, a second, and a third—in that order. It might have looked like we were going backward, but we were still leading in the points. But it was early in the season, and it wasn't much of a lead. Just 5 points.

Then at Rockingham on one of the coldest days I can remember in racing—it was 19 degrees when we started getting the car ready that morning—it finally happened. We blew an engine about halfway into the race.

Well, in those days NASCAR would let you change engines during a race. But just because it was legal, that didn't make it easy. You had to get it done fast to get your car back out on the track in time to finish the race. Cale came into the pits, and we took the car into the garage area and went to work on it. And we had it back out on the track in 36 minutes, so we still didn't have a DNF. People made a lot out of that, about how good we were as a crew, but we were actually *better* than that. For some reason—maybe it was the cold and being Southern boys, we weren't used to it—we were actually *slow* that day. Later that year, at Charlotte, we had another engine blow. That time, it took us only 13 minutes flat to put a new one in the car.

But as good as that time was, you'd actually rather *not* be proving to the world how quickly you can change engines. You want the first engine to hold up for the whole race because that's the way you win. We were winning races in '78, but we weren't doing it consistently—not like we'd done the 2 years before, especially not in the early part of the season.

If there was anything good that came out of that inconsistency, it was that it gave me a chance to get back on the other side of the wall and be part of the action on race day.

Like I said earlier, I'd done some tire changing before but had to quit doing that because my knee had a way of locking up on me when I really didn't need it to, like when we had to make a smooth, fast pit stop to win a race. So I stayed on the other side of the wall and let other people work on the car until, in the off-season, I had surgery to fix the knee.

But that didn't automatically get me back across the wall because the two guys Junior hired—Brewer and Carter—were both tire changers. Junior was the jackman. There wasn't a place for me, and I didn't know how I was going to get back over the wall to pit the car. And that's where the fun is.

Then, in one of those races when we'd dropped out of contention, Junior said to me, as we were getting ready to pit the car, "You take the jack on this one."

So all of a sudden I was doing the boss man's job. And he had a unique way of doing it, too, and he wanted me to use his technique. Junior never picked the jack up and ran around the car. He'd swing the jack around behind his back while he was on the run. It was a move that he'd made famous. It wasn't just show-off stuff; it saved time. But I'm here to tell you that it wasn't any easy thing. We didn't have aluminum jacks back then. They were steel and weighed about 75 pounds. So it took a little time and a few bumps and bruises in the afternoon, outside the garage, practicing until I had it down and knew I could do it in the heat of a race. But pretty soon, I could do it just like Junior.

And then, a lot of times, Junior would just give me the radio. Again, maybe we'd be down a lap, and he'd be getting frustrated. So he'd say to me, "Here, *you* talk to him."

So I'd put on the headphones, talk to Cale about how the car was handling and when did he want to come in and should he take two tires or four. That was Junior's way of letting me learn without putting me in harm's way. And it was also his way of telling me that he had confidence in me. I took advantage of it, and I'm still grateful.

So we were racing every weekend, and finally, at Darlington in April, we blew an engine so late in the race that we didn't have time to put a new one in and get back out on the track and finish the race. The streak of finishing every race that we started came to an end.

When we went back to the garage and got back to work, I think everyone was feeling a little frustrated. We were in a close points race, for one thing, against some tough competition. Dave Marcis was leading at one point that season. Bobby Allison was in there. Richard Petty, too. And so was the guy who was getting to be our biggest rival—Darrell Waltrip.

Waltrip had a good car and a good situation. He was under contract to the DiGard team—with Gatorade sponsorship—and it was a sweet deal for him. He was doing better, in terms of dollars, than drivers like Cale, who had won more races and more championships. Waltrip had won a few races, but he still hadn't won his first championship. But he was making more money—and more noise—than anyone.

It's hard, these days, to appreciate just how *different* Darrell Waltrip was in NASCAR back then. This was a sport that had its roots in the old, rural traditions where a man didn't run his mouth. He let his actions do the talking. People like Cale and Richard Petty, who were the heroes of the sport, were John Wayne sort of men who let their driving do the talking, out on the track. And after the race, they'd say a few words about how good the car was, how hard the crew worked for the victory, and how the other drivers out there had run a really good race. And that was it. They didn't run down the other drivers, and they didn't blow their own horns. That was just the way things were. It was almost a question of, you know, *values*.

Then here comes this kid from Owensboro, Kentucky, talking about how great he is and running down the other drivers and the other teams. And it isn't just what he says, it's that he won't let up. He is talking *all the time*.

We didn't like it, and other drivers and crews didn't like it. We're thinking, *Who does this motor mouth think he is? Richard Petty has won almost 200 races, Cale Yarborough has won two straight championships, and this guy is running them down. It ain't right.*

It wasn't that we just didn't like what Waltrip was saying. We didn't like that he was talking at all. And we wanted to shut him up in the worst way. Like I said earlier, it got to where there was nobody on the track I wanted to beat more than Waltrip, and I think everybody on just about every team on pit row felt the same way.

Now, all these years later, I realize that Waltrip was probably exactly the right personality at exactly the right time. In a funny way, he was what NASCAR needed. His style was more in tune with the spirit of those times than the old guard who were stoic and laconic and did their talking with race cars.

When you are trying to appeal to a mass market, you need big personalities, and sometimes you need controversial personalities. Just being a good athlete—and also a good driver in the case of NASCAR—wasn't necessarily enough to excite the interest of the casual fan or the person who might become a fan if he could get interested in a personality first.

When Muhammad Ali came along—even when he was still calling himself Cassius Clay—people didn't realize how much his kind of personality, and the controversy he sparked, appealed to people. There were millions of people who didn't care anything about boxing who got interested in it because of Ali. You had the same thing in other sports, like Joe Namath in football.

What I'm saying is that a colorful personality can be irritating to people up close, but it can bring excitement and new fans to your sport. I think Darrell did that, even though I didn't like it at the time, and I got mighty tired of his chin music.

In a lot of ways, 1978 was a year when NASCAR was starting to break the old molds and stereotypes and reach out to a broader audience. It was a turbulent time in the sport, and Darrell Waltrip was just one sign.

We had women driving, for instance. In 1976, Janet Guthrie had practiced and talked about trying to qualify for the Indy 500, and there had been a lot of press coverage about it. When she didn't make a qualifying attempt at Indy, one of the promotional geniuses of racing—Humpy Wheeler—had the idea that NASCAR should get her a ride in the 600-mile race at Charlotte on that same weekend so we could ride the wave of all that publicity she'd generated. He talked it up, and a vice president at the First Union Bank in Charlotte named Lynda Ferreri came up with enough money to pay for a ride. Guthrie qualified 27th for the race. She ran pretty good and finished 15th, which I thought was respectable. Some of the other drivers thought so, too.

Dave Marcis, who was already a veteran and went on to race longer than just about anyone, said, "NASCAR needs more rookies like her. She watched her mirror and got out of the way when faster cars were coming up on her. I think she's got enough experience to do a hell of a job."

But there were other drivers, including mine, who weren't so sure. Cale said, "She was trying to prove a point. Now she ought to go home."

Richard Petty was even harder on her. "My wife," he said, "could have done better with 14 screaming kids in the backseat."

I think Guthrie ran a good race, and she handled herself pretty well for the next couple of years while she was still racing. It was a tough deal. There were guys who supported her, but there were plenty who didn't, who thought of racing as a man's sport and didn't think women belonged in the cars, in the pits, or in the garage area. End of story. There weren't any women's bathrooms or locker rooms in the garage area, and that was just one of the ways Guthrie was made to feel unwelcome. There were things said behind her back that she was meant to hear or that got back to her. But she hung in and raced for a while, and a lot of the guys came around.

The funny thing is, there had been women in racing before she came along. It had just been so long that a lot of people had forgotten . . . if they ever knew. Sara Christian, a housewife from Atlanta, had run at Charlotte in the race that evolved into the 600, way back in 1949. She qualified 13th and drove the first part of the race. Bob Flock ran the rest of it, and they finished 14th. In another race, she came in 6th. That race was won by Curtis Turner, who was one of the great, hard-charging NASCAR legends and a plenty macho guy. He was so impressed by Sara Christian that he invited her to join him in Victory Lane.

So there had been female drivers in NASCAR before Janet Guthrie came along. And even though there was some resistance, there were also some visionaries—like Wheeler—who saw that there was a big segment of the population out there who would identify with a successful woman driver. So Guthrie had her supporters inside of racing and some of them were pretty influential. I kind of think R.J.

(continues on page 55)

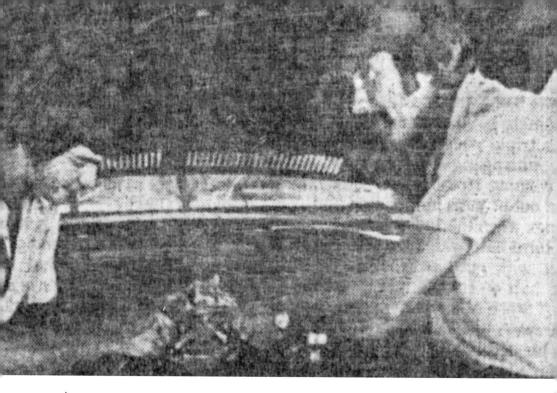

▲ *An early newspaper clip.*

▼ *The early days. Before I went with Junior Johnson, I crewed for Walter Ballard Racing with Tighe Scott driving the number 30 car. I'm in the top row, third from the left.*

▲ Darlington and my first trip to Victory Lane with the Junior Johnson racing team. That's me on the left in the front row.

▶ Handing Cale Yarborough his signature cavalry hat after his qualifying run at Charlotte in 1978.

▼ One of the legendary drivers, Cale Yarborough won three straight championships driving for Junior. No other driver had done it before and no driver has done it since.

◄ *Winners at North Wilkesboro. The crew, families, and friends. That's Junior Johnson holding the trophy. I'm kneeling on the left end of the front row.*

▼ *Cale Yarborough gets right-side tires at Charlotte in 1980. That's me on the jack.*

◀ *Winners at North Wilkesboro. The crew, families, and friends. That's Junior Johnson holding the trophy. I'm kneeling on the left end of the front row.*

▼ *Cale Yarborough gets right-side tires at Charlotte in 1980. That's me on the jack.*

Junior Johnson and his over-the-wall gang at the old Ontario, California, track in 1980.

▲ **With my wife, Sharon, at the Waldorf for an awards banquet. It was my first trip to New York.**

▼ **The Dew Crew gets it done. I'm the crew chief (the guy on the radio headset).**

Reynolds was pushing for a more inclusive image, too. And that made sense. So the next year, in the Firecracker 400 at Daytona, there were three female drivers competing: Janet Guthrie, Lella Lombardi, and Christine Beckers. There was a ceremony to honor the occasion, and Louise Smith, who had driven in the 1949 race at Daytona, was there for that.

Unfortunately, none of those three drivers finished the race that day.

The same year, 1978, Humpy Wheeler was at it again. This time he was trying to get a ride in the 600 for a driver named Willy T. Ribbs, a young African-American from California who'd had some success on road courses. Wheeler got an owner named Will Cronkrite to give Ribbs a ride in a Ford that had a good history. The car had won twice at Talladega so there was a lot of pre-race interest and coverage. It was the racial angle, of course, that was the story.

But, while it was certainly a good story, Ribbs wasn't NASCAR's first black driver. There had been a couple of others before him, and one of them, a guy named Wendell Scott, probably should have been named Rookie of the Year in 1961 for having five top-10 finishes in the 23 races he started. The driver who got the award only started five races, and he had one top-10. I was just a kid back then so I can't say for sure, but it does sound like a clear-cut case of prejudice. Scott won the race at Jacksonville in 1963, so he was the first African-American driver to win a NASCAR event. And he is still the only one.

Scott was an independent, driving against the factory-supported teams of the day, so he had to overcome more than just prejudice. He was always running on a shoestring, and he had to do some un-orthodox things just to keep racing. He'd do things like get out of the car and help the crew during pit stops because he didn't have enough money to pay for a full crew. Still, he had 1 year when he finished

10th in the points and another when he came in 14th. That's really strong when you consider what he was up against.

The best story about Scott is probably the one about how he blew the engine in his car in practice on the Saturday before a race at Martinsville. He was on a shoestring and wasn't traveling around with spare engines. So he took the engine out of his tow truck, put it in his car, and then went out and ran the race. He got lapped 64 times but still finished 16th.

After that race, Richard Howard, who was general manager at Charlotte, promised Scott a ride in the 600. Seems like these things were always happening at that race. Anyway, the car was a Junior Johnson Chevrolet, and it should have been a good deal, but the engine blew early. Still, there was ceremony honoring Scott at the race, and he was given the Curtis Turner Memorial Award for his contributions to racing.

So, like I say, Ribbs wasn't the first, but there was still a lot of excitement leading up to the '78 race. But there were problems. The team had two practice sessions scheduled so Ribbs could get used to the car and the track, but he was a no-show for both of them. Then he got arrested for driving the wrong way down a one-way street in Charlotte.

The way it wound up was that Ribbs didn't get the ride. Cronkrite fired him and went looking for a replacement driver. He settled on a local boy who seemed to have some talent and was doing all right on the dirt tracks but having trouble getting a ride in a Cup car. His name was Dale Earnhardt.

Dale didn't win the 600, but he did finish. He also spun his car with about 4 laps to go in the race. After the restart, Darrell Waltrip managed to get across the finish line ahead of everybody else. Cale was fourth, just a couple of seconds behind.

For me, and for everybody else on the team, that was the important thing. The stuff about Ribbs, women drivers, and the rest of it was just background noise. We'd just lost a close race to the driver we most wanted to beat, and we'd dropped behind, again, in the points.

We were defending our title and having a tough time of it. But there wasn't any quit in the team. One week after Waltrip beat us at Charlotte, Cale went out on the track in Nashville and was the first lap leader. At the end of the race, he was still leading. He led *every single lap* of that whole race. That almost never happens, and it kicked us back into the points lead. At the end of the race, Cale said, "We have the best team in stock car racing, despite what anyone says."

It's for sure that none of us was saying anything different. And even Darrell Waltrip was kind of quiet. He ran 26th and got a DNF. Rear end gave out on him.

But that was just one race, and we weren't halfway through the season. There was a lot of racing still to do. But we were running good again. No question about it. So good that after one race, at Michigan, we had people suggesting that maybe we were *too* good, that we were fast because we were illegal. David Pearson was saying, "They've got to be running a big engine. At the end of the race, he just runs off and leaves us."

Cale just said, "I'll leave the mouth racing to them."

We got through NASCAR's tear-down inspections all right. They didn't find anything illegal, and if they can't find it, it doesn't exist. We got the win at Michigan.

Pearson took the Firecracker from us at Daytona when Cale got held up by a slower car near the end. But we came back the next week at Nashville. That track was really good to us. This time, we led all but 9 laps. Cale said after the race that he could have led 'em all if he'd wanted to, but he was saving the car.

We weren't exactly coasting—Junior and Cale squabbled about a green flag pit stop at Talladega that might have cost us the race—but we weren't having the kind of public problems that other teams were having. This was the situation with Waltrip, especially, and we felt like it couldn't happen to a nicer guy.

About halfway through the season, Waltrip started complaining about his deal with DiGard Racing. He was only about 6 months into a very sweet 5-year contract, but that didn't seem to matter. He was unhappy, and he let everybody know about it. It was partly the money, I think, but more than that, too. Darrell wanted to be number one. When he walked down the street, he wanted people to point and say, "There goes the best driver that ever was." It is not unusual for a driver to have a big ego. Most of them do. They have to if they're going to do what they do. Darrell's ego was just bigger than most, and he wasn't shy about letting it show.

So Darrell thought something was holding him back. He figured it couldn't be his driving, so it must have been the situation he was in. He had to get out and get a new ride, he said, and he was pretty up front about where he planned to be the next season. Darrell said he was going to be driving Harry Ranier's Oldsmobile. The folks at DiGard had other ideas, and they threatened to enforce the contract with lawyers in every state where NASCAR raced.

Darrell didn't back down, either. He said he was "flat out" driving for Ranier the next season and that "whoever wants to sponsor the best darned team in racing had better get in touch with us."

Well, right then, Lennie Pond was Ranier's driver. Pond was a good driver, but he was having a tough season. He did win, though, at Talladega in early August. Then, a couple of weeks later, at Bristol, he and Waltrip start playing bumper cars. They got together, pretty hard, twice during the race. Pond said he didn't mean to get into Waltrip, but that he'd had a tire go flat on him after Darrell had gotten into him a few laps earlier. Harry Ranier made Pond park the car. He said he wasn't going to tolerate any grudge matches.

We won the race, by the way.

We won the next week, too, at Darlington. It was the Labor Day race, and that's a big one. What made it sweeter is that we were running close with Waltrip, and near the end, we both had to pit. He took four new tires. We just put in some fuel and kept racing. Waltrip blamed his pit crew for making him change tires.

"I knew if we took on tires, Cale wouldn't, and that he'd win easy," Waltrip said. "That decision came from the crew. I was too busy racing to make the decision for them."

Darrell won the next week, at Richmond, but he sure didn't make any new friends doing it. Near he end of the race, there were three cars nose to tail: Neil Bonnett, then Darrell, and then Bobby Allison. Darrell bumped Bonnett in turn one and kept getting into him until he had Bonnett into the guardrail. Allison got ahead for a couple of laps, but Waltrip caught him and won the race.

Bonnett was so mad that after the race, he drove down pit road and slammed his car into Waltrip's. The fans weren't too happy either. Waltrip needed a police escort to get to the press box for post-race interviews.

"I suppose Neil has a right to be upset," Waltrip said. "I guess I would be, too. But I try to win the race anyway I can. I don't like to be booed, but I'm not going to let it bother me, and it won't change the way I drive."

Darrell was just making friends all over the place.

Cale won back-to-back races at Martinsville and North Wilkesboro. Waltrip was second in both races. The one at North Wilkesboro was the kind that just sort of cuts the heart out of your opponent. Darrell had been leading every lap, and we were struggling with chassis adjustments. Darrell had to pit for new tires, and with 19 laps to go, we passed him for the lead. We ran 130 laps on one set of tires, and, once again, some people thought we were cheating.

"Our tires just wore out," Bobby Allison said. "This must have been another one of Junior Johnson's *miracles*."

I actually wish, after all the years, that I could reveal some secret, illegal scheme that got us that much distance on one set of tires. But the boring truth is, Travis Carter and Tim Brewer just worked hard to make the car handle right and get a setup that made the tires last. I suppose it proves that if you're good, you don't have to cheat.

We sewed up the championship at Rockingham in late October. We got our 10th win of the season, and Cale made it look easy. He led for the last 352 laps of the race and won by more than 2 laps. Most of the fans left before the checkered flag came out. They might have been bored, but we weren't. Cale had won the points race 3 straight years. Nobody had done it before, and nobody has done it since. So Cale was talking about trying to win more championships than anyone in racing. He knew he'd never catch Richard Petty in total victories. Petty was closing in on 200, but the racing schedule had been cut so far back from when Petty was piling up those wins that nobody was ever going to challenge him. But Petty had six championships, and Cale now had three. He felt like he could catch the King there and maybe even pass him.

The Cup race might have been over, but Darrell was still making news. In late October, he renegotiated with DiGard and signed another long-term contract. Everybody, including Darrell, was all smiles and claimed to be really happy, but some people wondered just how long that would last. Darrell had run a good season—he won six races and finished third in the points—but it wasn't good enough to beat us.

In fact, there were people in racing who believed nobody could beat us but ourselves. In the last race of the year, at Ontario, California, it looked like that might be true. We almost missed the start of the race out there. We had a distributor go bad on the pace

lap and had to get a push into the pits so we could make the change and be there for the start.

It was a minor thing, and we still finished second in the race. But it might have been an omen of things to come. We had some rough times ahead of us.

Daytona was bigger than ever that year, mainly because the race was going to be on live, network television, flag to flag, for the first time ever. CBS was giving 4 hours to showcase the biggest race on the NASCAR calendar. This was a long, long way from those days of racing on the beach in front of a few hundred fans, who were sitting in temporary bleachers or standing on the tops of their cars to get a better look. This race would be seen by millions.

It was raining on race day, and we got a late start and ran the first few laps under caution while the track dried. But when the green flag dropped, the racing started, and it was about as good as racing gets. The pole sitter, Buddy Baker, went out early, and then Cale Yarborough got into it with Bobby and Donnie Allison. Everybody went sliding into the infield where Cale got stuck in the mud. By the time he got back on the track, he was 3 laps down.

But we had a good car, and Cale got some cautions, and he kept fighting back until he was on the lead lap. He and Donnie were hooked up in the draft and pulling away from everybody. When the white flag came out, Donnie was leading, and as they came down the straight, Cale made the classic slingshot move and ducked down low to make his pass. But Donnie saw what was happening for the third time and dropped down to block the way. Cale kept going lower and lower on the backstretch, with Donnie following him down to block the way, both of them going more than 190 mph. Finally, Cale ran out of track and when his tires hit the infield, he lost it. The car sort of scooted back onto the track and smacked into Donnie. They banged off each other, then came together again and went into the wall, then spun down into the infield, and both cars died there. Richard Petty—who, of course, had been in a famous, similar duel with David Pearson when they were showing Daytona on tape delay—went by them to take the checkered flag. It was the first race Richard had won in 45 starts.

*Y*ou know how when you get off on the wrong foot, it can be so hard to get things right? How turning something around after a bad start can be one of the hardest things in this life? Well, that's what the 1979 season felt like to us. We were the same people, and we were still good. But we kept having trouble; we kept shooting ourselves in the foot.

It started in January when we wrecked a car in practice. It didn't seem like a big deal at the time. In racing you wreck cars, and you either fix them or build a new one and get back to racing. We had to build another one, and before Daytona we went to Riverside where we ran a respectable fourth. But that was tough because Darrell Waltrip won the race.

But we looked like we were back strong at Daytona and were going to win the race . . . right up until the last lap, when everything fell apart.

Meanwhile, after the checkered flag, back in turn three, Bobby Allison had slowed down, then stopped, to see if his brother was okay after the crash. Words got exchanged, as they say, and pretty soon, the Allison brothers and Cale were throwing punches, rolling around on the ground, and generally getting after it. And every bit of this was on live television—not just the finish of the race, which was among the most exciting ever at Daytona, or anywhere else, but also the fight. Even though NASCAR later made some disapproving noises about how this wasn't the kind of behavior it expected from its drivers and stuff like that, the truth was the viewers ate it up. This was *exactly* what they thought NASCAR was about: hard racing and no-holds-barred competition, right down to the checkered flag and some fistfighting afterwards. The broadcast got a 10.5 rating, which was far more than CBS was hoping for. That translated into about 16 million viewers. The race was up against an Olympics kind of competition that got a 9.4 rating and a golf tournament that did 5.5. NASCAR at Daytona had blown their doors off.

So it was a great race for the sport. But not so great for us. Cale thought he'd been robbed of a win. NASCAR agreed and put Allison on probation for the move that pushed Cale down into the infield. But that didn't change two facts: We'd wrecked the car, and we'd lost the race. We had a fifth, but we weren't happy when we got back to the shop and started getting ready to run the next race.

We got a week off when there was too much snow to race at Richmond. But that didn't cool Cale down. The next weekend, he and Donnie Allison got into it again at Rockingham, early in the race. Donnie was trying to get under Cale when they hit, so it was the reverse of what had happened on the last lap at Daytona. It turned into one of those wrecks that just gathers up all the cars around it and some of the drivers, including Waltrip, blamed Cale.

"Someone," Darrell said, "ought to drag Cale out of his car and whip his butt."

But Donnie said it was "just a racing accident," and, well, what are you going to do?

We also blew an engine in that race, but we got another in the car in less than 20 minutes. So we finished, but we were 80 laps off the pace and trailing Waltrip in the points.

So far we had wrecked more cars than we'd won races. We were not exactly getting off to a good start.

At Richmond the next weekend, Cale just stroked it—hung back and drove safe in the early laps, then stepped up and closed the deal—for our first win. We felt like maybe we were getting back on top of things, but after a couple of top fives in March, we went down to Alabama in April and were back to wrecking cars again at Talladega. Cale and Buddy Baker got into it, and the car was too smashed up to finish the race.

Dale Earnhardt won at Bristol in April. It was his first victory in Cup racing. He'd started only 16 races, and there wasn't any denying that he was a future star, maybe *the* future star. Some people were saying he was a better driver and had a brighter future than Darrell Waltrip, who everybody had been saying was the next great driver. You can imagine how Waltrip felt about that.

But the truth is, there was a changing of the guard going on about then in NASCAR. We were seeing a generation of great drivers in their last winning seasons. Richard Petty had won more races than anyone in the history of NASCAR, and he had won six championships—and counting. As the season played out, it would come down to Petty and Waltrip for the championship. But there was also a new Petty racing. Richard's son, Kyle, had won an ARCA race at Daytona back in February. That was like hitting .300 in triple-A baseball and proving to everyone that you are ready for the big

leagues. Before the season was over, Kyle would be driving in Cup races, against his dad.

Dale Earnhardt was one of the new breed, and while none of us could see it at the time, Cale Yarborough was part of the old breed. We were in the last year of the decade and the '80s were going to be different. You'd be hearing names like Petty and Yarborough, Baker and Pearson less and less. And you'd be hearing Waltrip, Earnhardt, Bill Elliott, and Rusty Wallace more and more.

In the April race at Darlington that year, this was all really plain to anyone who was looking. Darrell ran Petty down on the last lap, and they passed each other four times and swapped some paint before Waltrip won the race. But what might have been even more of a sign of things to come was something that happened in the pits.

David Pearson came in for tires and thought he was going to take only two. But the pit crew put on four, and before they could get the lug nuts tight on the left side, Pearson took off out of the pit. When the crew was saying, "Whoa," Pearson thought they were saying, "Go." Before he got back to the track, both wheels came off that side.

Now the Wood brothers had been the most successful team of the '70s, and David Pearson was one of the greatest drivers, no question, in the history of NASCAR. The first 2½ years that Pearson and the Woods brothers were teamed up, they won 23 big track races. In 1973, they entered 18 races and won 11 of them. That is just plain remarkable. Pearson never really ran a full schedule while he was with the Wood brothers. He'd already won three championships when he was running in every race. There's no telling how many he would have won if he had done that full-schedule driving for the Wood brothers. But everybody was happy running the limited schedule.

But they weren't happy after those wheels came off at Darlington. Evidently, there had been some problems before that, too. The Wood brothers let Pearson go later that week, and Leonard Wood said that the deal with the tires wasn't the reason. Pearson agreed that things had been building up but that the foul up at Darlington had "triggered it."

However it came down, it was a shock to people in racing. David Pearson, "The Silver Fox," was without a ride. That was hard to believe, and it got our attention. If Pearson could be gone when things started going bad, then it could happen to anybody.

We crashed again at Talladega in May, and I thought we were going to lose our driver as well as the car. Cale went spinning out of sight, after Buddy Baker lost it at the start/finish line and caused one of those big Talladega melees. Cale got out of the car in a hurry—maybe because he was worried about fire or, probably, just to see if the car could be fixed. Right at that same time, Dave Marcis got slammed by somebody, came sliding into Cale, and pinned him between the two cars. Cale was so sure that he'd lost his legs that he told Marcis to check for him. Dave said later that from the way Cale had screamed, he was sure that the crash had cut his legs off. And it would have, too, if the car had hit him just a little harder. It turned out that Cale was very, very lucky. He lost feeling in his legs for only a couple of days. But it was a very scary thing.

We got it right the next week at Nashville. That track always seemed to be good to us. Petty later claimed he'd won the race. He said he'd run at least 3 more laps than Cale, and Bobby Allison backed him. But NASCAR let the finish stand the way it was called. NASCAR gives and NASCAR takes away. That weekend, NASCAR was giving.

We got back to finishing, if not to winning, and we were still hanging around in the points, but it was looking pretty much like a race between Bobby Allison, Richard Petty, and Darrell Waltrip. When Waltrip won at Nashville—our track—in July, he went up by more than 200 points, and he was crowing.

"This is my hometown track," he said. "I've been hearing about how great Cale Yarborough is. Well now, maybe they'll say how great *I* am."

We didn't say anything. We just went out and won the next race. The race at Pocono was finished under yellow, and that made some people—especially Waltrip—mad. He ducked into the pits for tires, figuring he'd get a green, and it never came out. Tough luck.

The really hard-luck driver in that race was Dale Earnhardt, who blew a tire while he was leading and crashed so hard he fractured his collar bones and messed up his knee pretty badly.

A month later, the driver who replaced Earnhardt ran great at Darlington and won the Labor Day race. David Pearson had made up for losing two wheels when he was coming out of the pits. It was a great moment for him.

It wasn't such a great moment for Waltrip. He hit the wall. Twice. In the same place. He happened to be leading the first time. After the race, he said he was too embarrassed to go home. He thought he "might get a spanking." He could be funny with that mouth of his.

In mid-September, Petty won at Dover, and he was now breathing hard down Waltrip's neck. Waltrip had never won a championship, and Petty had won six. So you know it made Darrell think when Richard said, "The pressure is on him. I ain't got nothing to lose. Nobody expected me to be anywhere near the point lead."

Petty hadn't won a single race the year before. But that didn't mean he'd stopped being Richard Petty. That was one man you didn't want to see in your mirror, coming up to make the pass.

I don't know for sure if Darrell was feeling the pressure. But he did some things that made us think he was. At North Wilkesboro, he got into it with Bobby Allison and was black-flagged twice. He claimed he was just getting even with Allison for wrecking *him*.

"I can't believe he'd do something like that, knowing the point race I'm in," Darrell said.

The way people felt about Darrell, that might have been a reason for somebody to wreck him. But Allison claimed it wasn't like that at all. "He's got to learn that when you want to pass someone, you go around him. Not through him," Bobby said.

That race seemed to get to Darrell. Petty won the next week at Rockingham, and Darrell got black-flagged again, this time for leaving oil on the track. Petty went ahead in the points race, but Darrell came back the next week at Atlanta and was leading Petty by 2 points with one race to go.

"That means I'll have to beat him by just one position," Richard said, and he sounded plenty confident.

We were still racing, of course. Took a third at Atlanta and thought we had a pretty good car going out to California. We felt like we'd righted the ship, and maybe we'd get a win and set ourselves up for the next season.

We ran good but not good enough. Took third. Meanwhile, in the matchup everyone was watching, Darrell spun and got caught down a lap when a caution came out. He never made up the lap. Petty finished *three* places in front of him, in fifth, and became Winston Cup champion by 11 points. It was his seventh championship, so I guess you could understand that he was *disappointed*. Not with winning but with how he did it.

"I wanted to win the championship by winning the race," Richard said. "That's how it should be done."

That was the voice of the old generation of drivers talking right there. You always raced to win, and you always wanted to run out front.

Darrell was devastated. "I'm leaving with a broken heart," he said. "It's very depressing."

It felt strange going home being just one of the also-rans. This was my fourth year of Cup racing, and every year until now I'd gone home as part of the championship team. This season, after all we'd been through, we'd still finished fourth in the standings. We'd won four races. Had 19 top fives. Made pretty good money. Not a season to be ashamed of, for sure. And you know, in your mind, that you can't win them all. That you'll have days when things happen that you can't help. And, brother, we'd had plenty of those. Still . . . this was a different feeling.

But next year was a new season and a new decade, and I felt like we'd be back. It just took a little longer than I thought it would, and it would include a cast of characters I couldn't have ever imagined.

*T*he way it turned out, 1980 was a great year for us. We won six races—more than anyone else—and we had 19 top fives. We also had a better season than Darrell Waltrip, the driver who we thought was going to be our main competition for the Winston Cup. Waltrip had promised the world that he was going to come back and win the championship after he'd come so close the season before, and

we were looking forward to making him eat those words . . . and a lot of others besides. But what none of us realized was that we were going to be going up against a driver who had destiny on his side.

Dale Earnhardt had been NASCAR Rookie of the Year in '79. In 1980, he showed the world that his rookie season hadn't been any fluke and that the racing world had better pay attention because he was going to be around, and he was going to be winning races. Early in the season, Richard Petty was close to Earnhardt in the points, but then Petty crashed at Pocono and broke his neck. Petty came back and drove in some more races and finally wound up his career with 200 wins. But he never won another championship. He had seven when he retired, and he was, without a doubt, a NASCAR legend. Only one other driver has won seven championships—Dale Earnhardt, who is also a legend. The 1980 season was the first chapter of that story.

Now, I'd known Dale for some time. We'd first met when he was working on his dad's car at Concord Motor Speedway. I remember Dale trying to argue with his dad and how Ralph Earnhart put him in his place in no uncertain terms. When Ralph said something, he meant for Dale to listen to him right then, and I think that wore off and helped make Dale what he became.

Like I said earlier, we actually tried to get Dale to drive for that car my uncle and I were running. We never were able to put the deal together, unfortunately, but Dale and I got to be friends, and I remember watching him early in his career, driving on dirt. He was something to see, and you could tell he had it, even back then. Dale might not have been quite as smooth as his dad, but he was aggressive as all get out. That was one thing he was never short of and it never changed. Even when Dale did get smoother and smarter behind the wheel, he was still the Intimidator.

As he moved along in his career, Dale and I remained good friends. I was working for Junior Johnson when Dale started winning a little and making some money. He'd bought himself a place down on Lake Norman, and I'd go down there and visit him. It was just a bunch of people hanging around. We'd drink Jack Daniels, go water-skiing, and play a little poker. Dale was really big on playing poker. I remember coming close to drowning Dale Jr. several times. He was one of those kids who just seemed to like to aggravate you and get on your nerves when you were playing cards.

There was one weekend after we'd been up to a race in Bristol and Cale had won. We drove back—Dale in his pickup with Teressa before they'd gotten married—and me in my car with my wife trying to keep up with him. Earnhardt was driving like he always did—wide open—and I don't believe I've ever made it down highway 77 so fast—before or since. What really got me about that trip was how he'd let us pass him, and then he'd come up on our bumper in that pickup and give us a little tap, right out on the highway, wide open. That was Earnhardt's idea of fun, wide open and tapping bumpers all the way back from Bristol where he'd just been in a race.

I remember another time when we were up at Bristol. We'd gotten rained out, and there wasn't anything to do but hang around and wait for the race. I was down in the garage, working on the car, when Dale came by and asked, "Hey, man, you hungry?"

I said, "Yeah, I could eat something."

"Well, you got a car?"

"No, but Junior does."

Junior said he didn't want to go get something to eat, but he gave me the keys to his brand-new, 4-door Impala, and a bunch of us went into town with Earnhardt driving. And he was getting after it. It had been raining, and the back-country roads were slick. Dale was sliding it around the turns and being Earnhardt.

We found us a little Chinese place in town and had lunch, and it got time to go back to the track, Earnhardt said, "Hey, Hammond, you want to drive back."

"Sure," I said, "I'll drive."

"Well you got to drive it just like I did coming over. You got to get after it."

Of course, right away, I'm thinking *challenge*!

"Yeah, okay," I said. "Let's do it."

So I'm sliding it around the corners on this wet pavement and generally getting after it when we come to a real hard left-hander and the front end starts pushing. I can't get it to come around so at the last minute, I touch the brake and the front snaps around and we go into the ditch.

I'd gotten it slowed up enough to where it just barely went over the edge. The car was literally standing up on its nose with the rear end up in the air and the tires off the ground so we can't go anywhere.

Well, Earnhardt was just cracking up and I was wondering what I was going to do about getting Junior's car out of the ditch, and how I was going to explain to him how I let Dale Earnhardt goad me into wrecking it. And, then, here comes the sheriff.

First thing out of Earnhardt's mouth was, "Big black dog, boys. Big black dog. That's the story. A big black dog ran out in front of us, and we went into the ditch to keep from hitting him."

So the sheriff got out and recognized Dale, who fed him the big black dog story and said, "Anything you can do to help us out."

So the sheriff drove Dale back to where he had his pickup parked, and he drove back with a chain he had and we pulled Junior's Impala out of the ditch. Cars were built a lot more durable back then so it wasn't too bad. But I had wrinkled some sheet metal and busted a headlight.

And I didn't much like going back to the track and telling Junior I'd wrecked his car.

I didn't have to worry, though, because Dale got there first and told everyone all about it.

I told Junior I'd pay to get his car fixed, and he just said, "Well, you take care of it."

Then, for the rest of the weekend, every time Earnhardt saw me, he'd start saying, "Big black dog. Big black dog." Then he'd just laugh.

Dale had a sense of humor . . . on most things, anyway.

But he was serious as a heart attack about racing, and after we'd been competing for a while, there were some incidents—especially one at Richmond that I'll get to later—that strained things between me and Dale. We stayed friends, but it wasn't like it had been. Then, late in my career as a crew chief, when I'd started doing some broadcasting, we patched it up.

Part of my job was interviewing drivers, and the producer wanted me to talk to Earnhardt so I found him at the track and said I'd like to sit down sometime and interview him for the show.

"Yeah," he said, "we can do that. Why don't you come up to the farm. But you got to be there early. And I mean *early.*"

We're talking 5:30 in the morning, so I got up in the dark and drove out to his farm. When I got to his office in the shop there, Dale was sitting at the desk with some reading glasses perched on his nose. He was answering his fan mail and signing autographs. Turned out, that was his ritual. He'd do that early in the morning when there wasn't anything else going on to distract him. He stayed caught up that way.

We did the interview, and Dale was really helpful and sincere, and I got some good answers. Near the end of the interview, he said something about how we'd been friends for a long time and how much it meant to him. That just made all that other stuff go away.

When I was getting ready to leave, he said, "You know what, man, we need to go hunting sometime."

I told him I'd like that, and we sort of generally agreed that when we both had some time, we'd do it.

Of course, we never got the chance. I still can't believe that he's gone, and I sure do miss him.

* * *

That 1980 season, when Dale won his first championship, was actually pretty exciting both on and off the track. We had a lot of good races, and the points race went down to the very end and was one of the closest in NASCAR history. Darrell Waltrip got into another contract squabble and was in the news for running his mouth, which was nothing new. We sort of expected that. But Earnhardt's team went through some turmoil, too, and that was kind of surprising because they were winning. In racing, when something ain't broke, generally you don't fix it.

That was Junior's way of thinking, and things seemed pretty much under control on our team with Tim Brewer and Travis Carter as co-crew chiefs. That's the way it seemed to me, anyway. But sometimes there are things going on under the surface that you don't know about. Turned out that's what was happening with us, and pretty soon it was going to feel like the walls came crashing down on us.

We started slowly. Got a DNF at Riverside where Darrell won the race and got a leg up on delivering on his promise to win the Cup. But Earnhardt was a close second. Then Waltrip blew an engine at Daytona and started ragging on his team, saying it wasn't "a bit better than when I joined in 1975."

Waltrip's DiGard team had fired Buddy Parrott as crew chief after the '79 season and then hired him back about 6 weeks later. After Daytona, it looked like Parrott might be on the hot seat again.

We had our own troubles at Daytona. Cale Yarborough crashed early, but we figured that was just racing. There wasn't any scapegoating.

Earnhardt, by the way, finished fourth at Daytona. He ran a good race, but he just couldn't quite catch Buddy Baker. He'd come close the year before, too, and might have won the race if he hadn't had a bad pit stop. The Daytona 500 turned into the jinx race for Earnhardt over the rest of his career. He came close a lot of times, but fate just seemed to keep getting in his way. He was leading late one year when a tire went flat. And another time, when he was out front, he actually hit a seagull. It didn't seem right that one of the greatest drivers in history couldn't win NASCAR's biggest race.

Earnhardt came out of Daytona ahead in the points, and he held onto that lead like a bulldog with something in his teeth. He wasn't going to let go no matter who chased him or how hard. And, of course, that was his driving style. Sometimes it just seemed like he had more will than any other driver on the track.

We weren't scared, though, and we weren't quitting. We got a win at Rockingham in our backup car. The finish order of that race was sort of like a roster at the changing of the guard ceremony. First— Cale Yarborough. Second—Richard Petty. Third—Dale Earnhardt. Fourth—Darrell Waltrip.

Atlanta in April was even more of a sign of things to come. Earnhardt won there. It was his first superspeedway victory, and he had to come from way back in the pack to do it after he'd had a bad qualifying. But there was also another sensational young driver on the track that day.

Rusty Wallace was 23 years old and looked like he was maybe 15. He didn't look old enough to have a driver's license, much less to be making his first Winston Cup start. Rusty had this big head of frizzy red hair and a sweet, innocent smile, but he was an assassin in a race car. The kid could flat-out drive. Rusty was smooth, like Waltrip, and he understood the car and how to keep it together on the track. Plus, he was driving for Roger Penske, who was trying to succeed in NASCAR the way he had at Indy racing. You knew if you were driving for a Penske team that you were part of an outfit that was all about winning.

And Rusty ran a great race. Came in second to Earnhardt. So Waltrip, who had been the sensation, was looking at more competition. And he had a bad weekend at Atlanta. First, he got booed during the driver introductions. And then when his car broke down and he had to leave the race, the crowd cheered.

"Why do these people hate me?" Darrell asked, making like he didn't get it. And maybe he didn't. But with his mouth and arrogance, he'd made himself into the driver you loved to hate. People wore T-shirts that read: *Warm Beer, Cold Women, and Darrell Waltrip.*

But there was no denying that Darrell could drive a race car. He won his third race of the season, at Martinsville in April; then he lost to Benny Parsons by half a car length in the 600 at Charlotte. Earnhardt crashed in that race but was still barely leading in the points race on Monday morning when his crew chief, Jake Elder, quit on him over some problems he was having with the team manager.

Meanwhile, Buddy Parrott had been fired again over at DiGard, and the way I heard it, he went looking for people in the shop. He found Robert Yates and smacked him upside of the head. He was looking for Waltrip, too, wanting to do the same to him, but he never found him. He did tell the press that he'd "never turn a wrench on a Darrell Waltrip car again," and I don't believe anyone in the whole racing world doubted him.

Jake Elder went over to Waltrip, but Darrell was still unhappy with his situation at DiGard, even though he had already renegotiated his contract once. He kept up the complaining all through the season, and it was sort of amusing from a distance. There was starting to be some tension in our shop, too, with the co-crew chief arrangement. And there were rumors about other teams wanting to come in and take some of our people away, which made sense because we'd won three championships in a row. If you want to build a successful organization fast, you steal people from one that is already winning.

I was aware of the rumors, of course, but I didn't take them too seriously. Since I'd been with Junior, there hadn't been that many changes. Herb Nab's leaving was the biggest, and I figured Herb probably regretted it now, because he was on the outs at his new team and wasn't even in the shop or at the track, even though he was still under contract. We heard that the team owner had him cleaning bricks at a construction site to earn his salary.

Anyway, I thought Junior's operation was like a sort of island of stability in this sea of NASCAR turmoil. But it turned out I was about as wrong as I could possibly be.

We didn't really have time for that. We were in a race with Earnhardt for the points championship. He took one from us at Nashville, a track that had been good to us. But we got him at Bristol and closed the gap to 23 points.

It was now August, and we started falling a little farther and farther behind Earnhardt. Things were feeling different in the shop. I believe that as hard as we tried not to be, we were all distracted by the rumors about big changes coming and the feeling that something was happening that kept getting stronger and stronger. We just had this sense that things were coming to a point, and I think that caused us to lose focus a little bit. And in racing, a little bit can be a whole lot.

Then, in early September, the bombshell hit. Cale Yarborough announced that he was leaving Junior Johnson to drive for M.C. Anderson. And what made it worse was talk that our new driver would be none other than Darrell Waltrip.

I took it hard. This was the only team I'd worked for full-time. Cale had been my only driver, and I looked up to him and respected him as much as any man in the world. He was my idea of what a winning NASCAR driver should be, and I couldn't imagine how anyone could come in and replace him behind the wheel of the number 11 car.

I especially couldn't imagine *Darrell Waltrip* doing it. Waltrip hadn't just been our rival those past 3 years. He was the enemy. We'd had to put up with his mouth—calling us cheaters and all sorts of other things—even when we were beating him. Most of us didn't want to have anything to do with him, except to wave to him as we went by on our way to Victory Lane.

It was just one of those things that happens in sports, where you can't imagine a certain person changing colors. Like when Roger Clemens ended up pitching for the Yankees. If you were a Red Sox fan, you thought to yourself, "Man, anybody but the Yankees." And if you were a Yankees fan, your first thought was, "Man, anyone but Clemens." Well, after we heard the rumors, all of us in the shop were thinking, "Oh, man, anyone but *Waltrip.*"

I was young back when that all happened, and it really shocked me. I didn't realize just how much of what we were doing was a business and how important the money was. Now I can understand Cale's thinking. He was getting a little burned out, racing every week, year after year, and he was thinking to himself, "Man, I have won three championships, and what have I got to show for it?"

Cale was making good money, by the standards of the time. I imagine he was getting paid $100,000 to drive for Junior, plus a cut of the purses and some appearance money. But he looked around and there were other drivers, under long-term contracts, who were getting paid more, and they hadn't won *any* championships. And now, with NASCAR's popularity growing so fast, thanks to television and other things, there were more people coming in and waving checkbooks around and promising people more money than they ever thought they'd make racing. You can't blame them for wanting to take advantage of the opportunity. It's like when free agency came to baseball. Suddenly you weren't just talking about more money; you were talking about a *lot* more money.

So Cale saw the chance to go out and make the kind of money that, say, Darrell was making, and he took advantage of it. He was also talking about running a more limited schedule, instead of entering every race and chasing the points championship. He had a family, and he wanted to spend more time with them on his farm. In hindsight, the only reaction seems to be, "Sure. What's the problem?"

But that isn't the way I took it back then. And it sure wasn't the way Junior took it. Junior was a businessman, and he was in racing to make money. He felt that if he made a deal with someone then they had a deal. And if for some reason, they weren't happy with the deal and wanted to be somewhere else, then he felt, "Hey, don't let the doorknob hit you in the ass on the way out." Junior didn't renegotiate after a deal had been made. And he didn't get to be successful by making deals that were bad for him.

And like everyone in racing, Junior had his pride. Junior has said that he never saw another driver he didn't think he could beat, either when he was racing or after he quit. He wasn't in awe of any driver. When Cale said he was leaving, Junior's first reaction was, "Okay, then, we'll just win with another driver."

Benny Parsons had been driving for M.C. Anderson, and now that Cale was replacing him next season, Benny would obviously be out of a ride.

I remember Junior said to me, "Okay. That's it, then. Let's go get Benny and bring him up here. We'll finish with him, and we'll *still* win the championship. Benny was running third at the time, and we were second behind Earnhardt. It may be that we could have gotten it done—Junior keeping his owner points and Bennie keeping his driver points—but it just wasn't practical to make the switch right then, with the season almost over. But that's how Junior thought. It was a team effort, and it was his team. Nobody was indispensable— not even one of the greatest drivers in the history of the sport.

Cale wound up finishing the rest of the season for us, and it was an uncomfortable situation. It didn't sit well with Junior, and the two of them pretty much ignored each other in the garage area and the pits during practice and on race day. It changed the mood of things and was a distraction, that's for certain. Even all these years later, I still believe that had something to do with our not winning the championship that year. We came so close, just that little loss of focus might have made the difference.

But nobody could say that Cale Yarborough wasn't a warrior. After Earnhardt won back-to-back races at Martinsville and Charlotte, we were 115 points down with three races still to run, and it was looking pretty bleak.

We went to Rockingham in October with a lame-duck driver, a disgruntled owner, and a team that was distracted by the rumors about who would be driving for us next year. Cale won the race and cut Earnhardt's lead by more than half. We went to Atlanta the next week, and Cale led for three-quarters of the race. Earnhardt went down a lap, but that didn't keep him from crowding Cale at the end of the race. But Cale wasn't the kind of driver to back down. He took the checkered flag, and we went out to California just 29 points behind and looking to catch up. There was a feeling on the team that we wanted to put all the hard feelings of the last couple of months behind us and finish, not just the season, but a whole era, on a high note. We wanted badly to win the race and another championship.

But, like they say, you don't always get what you want in this life. We came close. We even got some help from Earnhardt's crew when they had some miscommunication and he went out of the pits too quickly. There were only two lug nuts on one tire, and he got black-flagged and lost a lap.

Cale ran good but not good enough. He finished third. Earnhardt was fifth, and he won the Cup by 19 points—4,661 to 4,642. Benny Parsons, who won the race, was third in the points and out of his ride in the M.C. Anderson car. Cale was moving over there, and that

left me feeling like a lot more than just another racing season was ending.

When it first came out about Cale leaving, the team didn't really know what to expect. We did know that Junior Johnson wasn't going to have any trouble finding somebody to drive for him. And we knew that it would be somebody good. We all knew Junior, and most of us had been working for him for a while, but I can't honestly say we knew how his mind worked. He was always thinking a little bit ahead of everyone else, and he would surprise us. I did know that he wasn't going to do something impulsive. Whoever he settled on to be his new driver, he was going to think about it, and he was going to have some good reasons for his decisions.

Around the shop, we heard him talking about two possibilities— Darrell Waltrip and Dale Earnhardt.

I don't know exactly how Junior went about making up his mind. Both of them were obviously great drivers. When he asked me how I'd feel about Waltrip driving for us, I'd say something like, "Well, I don't know . . . I'm not sure," and stuff like that. But what I was thinking is, *Man, I don't want that mouthy son of a gun coming in here.*

I had my mind made up about Waltrip, and I knew Dale Earnhardt. We were friends, and I knew we could work together. When I thought about him coming to drive for us, I could see championships all the way to the horizon.

But Junior saw things realistically, and he saw that Darrell was *ready*. That was the main reason, I think, that Junior went with Waltrip. He wanted a driver who had put the years of wrecking cars, doing dumb things, and being too aggressive behind him. Like I say, Junior ran a money-making operation. He wanted a winner, but he wanted someone who was thinking during a race about how he could get the most out of the car, stay in the race and finish and maybe win, and not just go as hard as he could until he drove the car into the ground. I believe that Junior thought that Darrell was more seasoned and that after coming close a couple of times and being disappointed that he was both ready and *hungry.*

I didn't see it that way, and I don't believe any of my teammates did, either. But, as usual, Junior was right. Darrell wanted to win as badly as any of us. It just took us a while to figure it—and him—out.

I've got a picture, somewhere, of me and Darrell sitting in a golf cart at the Ontario track before that last race in 1980. There is something a little bittersweet about that picture because it was taken at one of the last races they ever ran at that great track. For some reason, good as the facility was, people wouldn't come out to watch racing there. Even for a race to determine who would win the Winston Cup, only about 15,000 people showed up. Not long after that race, the track was sold to Chevron Oil, and they said they were going to tear it down. You can't ever forget the money part of racing.

But we were still racing at Ontario on the day that picture of me and Darrell was taken. I was sitting in that golf cart, talking to him— or trying to—because Junior had told us all that we'd better get used to having Darrell around because it looked like he was going to be our driver next season. There were still some legal details that had to be worked out to get Darrell out of his contract with DiGard, but more and more it was looking like a done deal.

We were going to be racing with the enemy.

I don't remember much of what we said to one another that day, sitting in that golf cart. I do remember that I didn't come away from that meeting feeling any better about things. It was really clear that Darrell Waltrip wanted things done Darrell Waltrip's way and that he didn't plan on doing a lot of compromising or meeting anyone halfway. He wasn't any more soft-spoken or any less opinionated than he'd ever been. When Darrell finally got out of his contract with DiGard, instead of being gracious, he started talking about how he

was "a free man" and how "if only the hostages in Iran will be set free, my world will be in good shape."

So even though Darrell said he didn't want to ever be in a long-term deal again, he signed a 3-year contract to drive for Junior. I believe Junior had decided that this was the way racing would be going, and he didn't want to be losing his driver in the middle of a championship run ever again.

Waltrip said that when he was a kid, Junior had been his hero and that to drive for Junior was the dream of a lifetime.

There were some of us who were thinking that maybe this whole thing was just a bad dream and that when the next season started, we'd wake up.

No such luck.

*T*he 1981 season was tougher, maybe, than any I ever went
through. It was both a good time and a bad time and also a time
when I had to suck it up and learn how to handle some things that I
didn't necessarily like. But I was going to have to deal with them if I
wanted to stay with Junior Johnson ... and maybe even keep my career in NASCAR alive. I wouldn't want to go through that season

again, but I'm grateful for having done it.

The '81 season would have been a challenge even if we hadn't
been dealing with the personnel changes. Cale Yarborough had
moved on, and Darrell Waltrip had replaced him, of course. Travis
Carter had also left the team. He became crew chief for the Skoal
Bandit ride that was put together by Hal Needham, the movie producer, and Burt Reynolds, the actor. Their driver was originally Stan
Barrett, but Harry Gant replaced him.

With Travis gone, Tim Brewer was now our sole crew chief.

So we had a new driver and a different crew chief arrangement—and that would have been enough of a challenge, right there. But on top of that, like everyone else, we were dealing with some of the most drastic rules changes in the history of NASCAR.

We'd all known, for years, that we were going to be changing to the smaller cars that Detroit was building. The rules had allowed for older cars, and in the 1980 season, there were even some 1977 models still winning races. But after the first race of 1981, we all had to go to the newer, smaller cars with a 110-inch wheelbase instead of 115 inches, which is what we were used to.

So during the off-season, everybody started taking these cars out to the track and testing them. We realized right away that we had our hands full. Drivers were complaining that the cars simply weren't stable. So NASCAR kept changing the rules on the size of the spoilers, and we were all experimenting with tires and various setups. By the time we got to Daytona, we felt like we had a handle on things. Sure enough, Darrell won the 50-mile Busch Clash Invitational and then took the second 125-mile qualifying race.

But in the first of those qualifying races, two different cars had just about gotten airborne when the drivers lost control. It was *scary* to look at, these 3,700-pound cars sailing like they were scraps of paper in the wind. It got a lot of people's attention.

The day after the qualifying races—that is, the Friday before the big race on Sunday—NASCAR increased the allowable area on the spoilers again. Everybody wanted to keep those cars down on the track where they belonged.

Even before the rules changes, we felt like we had a good car and a good chance. We'd been disappointed out in California, at Riverside, in the first race. Darrell had taken the pole and was leading early. But he missed a turn and went off the track, and then we had to change a fouled plug. That stop took almost 2 minutes. Darrell finished 17th, 11 laps down. And he wasn't shy about his feelings after the race.

But even before the race, Darrell was complaining about the car and how it wasn't *exactly* the way he wanted it. We'd never gone in for a lot of flashy stuff. When Cale was driving for us, we painted the inside of the car flat black and that was it. But Darrell had his image to keep up. He wanted the inside of the car painted the same color scheme as the outside, and he wanted us to buff all the aluminum surfaces and to do some other cosmetic stuff like that. The crew didn't like doing it, and we didn't like being told to do it. So we had a problem right from the get-go.

Now, we didn't like Darrell in the first place, and we thought we might know more about getting a car ready for a race than he did. After all, we'd been beating him for a few seasons now. But Darrell kept wanting things changed, and he'd push and push until we'd make the changes. We didn't necessarily like doing it, but we'd do it. I'm sure that one of the reasons we resented it was that we were so used to Cale's style, where he wouldn't try to micromanage what we were doing. Like I said earlier, Cale would tell us, "Boys, just get it close, and I'll make up the difference."

With Darrell it was, "Do this. Do that. Why can't you get it right?"

After a while, I'd start getting back in his face and saying, "The car is fine, so why can't you just *leave it alone*?"

But Darrell was the driver, and we tried to make the car the way he wanted it. So it was do this and do that and work and work and more work. There didn't seem to be any point to a lot of it. The only reason we were doing things was because Darrell wanted it.

To put it plain, Darrell was a pain in the ass.

At Daytona, after winning the Clash and the 125-Qualifier, we blew an engine and got a DNF in the big race.

By now, none of us around the shop was feeling too great. We were wondering if maybe we weren't seeing the shape of the season in the problems we were having in those first two races. Sometimes you seem to get in a slump, and it becomes impossible to get out of it. We didn't need that.

Then we got back-to-back wins at Richmond and Rockingham, and that made things a little better. We beat Cale by a couple of seconds at Rockingham, which made it a little sweeter. And it got even better when the other drivers started complaining about how long we ran on one tank of gas.

"I thought when Cale left Junior, he took that big gas tank with him," Bobby Allison said. "Looks like Junior still has it."

The tank was inspected before and after the race, and it was legal both times. If we were cheating, we were doing a good job of it. And I *still* say we weren't cheating. No more than anyone else, anyway.

Winning generally makes things right but not with us. Darrell didn't change his way of dealing with us, and we didn't suddenly like him any better just because he'd won a couple of races. The atmosphere around the shop was poisonous.

But it was a year when loyalty was being tested all over NASCAR. We were all seeing the effects of lots of new money coming into the sport. Probably the most shocking thing happened early in the season. The day after Richard Petty won the big race at Daytona, Dale Inman, who'd been his crew chief through some of his greatest seasons, quit to go to work for Dale Earnhardt and more money. Petty and Inman was one of those collaborations you sometimes have in sports where its seems like each guy makes the other one better. The way people around football thought about Joe Montana and Jerry Rice—that's the way racing folks looked at Inman and Petty.

But the money was hard to resist, and that winning partnership broke up.

After Charlotte, Darrell had won four races and was trailing Bobby Allison by about 250 points. And he was still about as popular with those of us on the team as he was with the fans. He and I had gotten into a couple of shouting matches, and things were to the point where I could hardly stand to talk to him anymore. If I had something to communicate to him, I'd say to it Brewer and let him argue with Waltrip. Because I knew that's what it would be—an argument. And I was sick of arguing with Darrell.

We were racing in Texas the next week, at College Station. This was another great track that never seemed to fill up. We knew we had fans in Texas, but for some reason they wouldn't come out to that track. NASCAR stopped racing there, finally.

But that wasn't my problem. I had my hands full dealing with our driver.

During the time we were getting ready for the race, Junior came over to talk to me in the garage area.

"What's the problem?" he asked.

"I don't know," I said. "Whatever we do, Waltrip wants it done the other way. And then, when we do it the other way, he wants it put back the way it was. We can't ever get it right, and it is getting to where I just can't stand dealing with him."

Junior nodded and said, "Well, we can't keep going on like this. I can't solve all these problems between you and Darrell and Tim and Darrell and still have time to do what I need to do. It's tearing up this team."

"Yes sir," I said. "I know."

"Seems to me," he said, "that we need to make some changes."

I nodded. I didn't know what was coming. I thought I might even get fired.

"Why don't you stop coming to the track?" Junior asked. "Let Tim handle things here and deal with Darrell. I want you to stay at the shop and work on the cars and make sure they're ready to race."

What Junior did, besides doing me a favor, was create the first situation where you had both a car chief and a crew chief, which is the way just about everybody does it these days. I took this responsibility and ran with it. I went to work with my guys at the shop, building cars and making sure we had a good car for whatever race we were running. I stopped traveling with the team and dealing so much with Darrell, and it made things a lot better.

The week after Junior started this new arrangement, Darrell won at Riverside in a car we'd built especially to run road courses. We'd moved all the chassis offsets and had the car set up specifically for the course we'd be running. We were ahead of our time, once again.

By mid-July, we'd won six races, and after we'd won a disputed race at Pocono, it was starting to look like we had a chance to run down Bobby Allison. We were just a little more than 100 points behind him, and we had a dozen races left.

Junior told us, "Boys, don't think about the points. Think about winning races. Do that and the points will take care of themselves."

So Darrell went out and started winning races. He won at Richmond in mid-September, and that put us just 3 points behind Allison. It looked like he was doing the same thing to Allison that Petty had done to him a couple of year earlier. Darrell was the hunter, and Allison was the hunted. Darrell was running to win, and Allison was trying not to lose.

Then, starting at Richmond in late September, Darrell won four races in a row. It was the first time anyone had done that since 1976. The driver who did it then was Cale Yarborough, back in my first year working for Junior.

In the last of those four races, Darrell and Bobby Allison raced about as hard as two drivers can race. They kept passing each other and swapping the lead. In the last 43 laps, they traded the lead five times. Darrell ran a great race, no question, and after he finished second the next week at Atlanta, all we had to do was go out to Riverside and stay out of trouble.

Darrell had the pole at Riverside where he ran a nice, conservative sixth and won the points race over Bobby Allison by 53 points. After the race,

Darrell told the reporters that, "Every time I'd get to running harder, Junior would come on the radio and say, 'Take care of that car, boy.'"

When Darrell heard Junior's voice, he did what he was told. That was the voice of authority, man, and it didn't just save the car in that race. It had saved the team, our whole season, and won us another championship.

Like I said before, when Junior Johnson talked, you listened.

In the end, the toughest, most stressful season I'd ever been through wound up being one of the most successful. When all the dust had settled, the number 11 car had won 12 races—more than one out of every three races we started. The next closest car—Bobby Allison's—had won five.

Instead of waiting until the next season to have the awards dinner at Daytona, like we'd always done, NASCAR had a ceremony in New York at the Waldorf-Astoria. It wasn't as fancy as it eventually got to be. We weren't in the Grand Ballroom that night, and we weren't wearing tuxedos—just business suits. And everybody didn't get these sort of Super Bowl–like rings the way they do now. We got belt buckles and plaques— which was a step up from the jackets we'd gotten at the Daytona cere- monies. And, of course, the food at the Waldorf was better than the tough roast beef we were served in the hotel basement in Daytona.

But the whole thing was pretty special, and it would have been great, no matter where they'd had the ceremony, because we were the cham- pions again. It was not the same as it had been in 1976 when I started with Junior and we were all like one big, happy family. Since then, Herb Nab had left. And then Cale had left. Darrell had come aboard and now, in this off-season, Tim Brewer told Junior he'd be leaving to go to M.C. Anderson, along with Harold Elliott, who was our engine builder, and Eddie Thrap, our fabricator. Anderson had decided the quickest way to get a team as good as Junior Johnson's was to buy Junior Johnson's team.

I realized that I had some thinking to do. And some growing up to do. So I went to Junior and told him I wanted to talk.

I went to talk to Junior Johnson because with Tim Brewer gone, the job of crew chief was open. I wanted that job—wanted it bad—and I thought I was ready to handle it. After going through a season where I could barely stand to talk to our driver and even had to stop going to the track with him for races, that probably sounded crazy, even to me. But I was convinced. Maybe putting some distance be-

tween me and Darrell had allowed me to study things a little and think about them more clearly without my ego and pride getting involved. I honestly thought I could work with Darrell and that together we could keep on winning races and championships.

I was still young back then—I wasn't even quite 25 years old—so it could also have been that I'd done some growing up and maturing during the last months of the season. That generally happens when you get married.

I'd met Sharon during the middle of the 1980 season when I went to pay my cable TV bill. I must have been late paying it because I went to the office instead of putting a check in the mail. My life was pretty chaotic, in those days, and I was on the road—either on my way to a race or coming back from one—a lot of the time.

I was living in Statesville, North Carolina, at the time, which is about halfway between Charlotte and Ronda. That way I didn't have to drive too far either to get to work or to visit my parents. And when I did want to go out, maybe date someone, I wasn't too far from Charlotte where most of the people my age lived.

But the cable offices were in Statesville, and the woman who took my check there was a really good-looking blonde with a great smile. I must have just come back from a race in either Texas or California because I remember I was wearing a cowboy hat when I went into the office.

I was still thinking about that woman when I got home and thought I'd like to try to get to know her, so I called the cable office. I introduced myself to the woman who answered the phone and explained that I'd just been in the office to pay my bill.

"Yes, sir," she said. "I hope there's nothing wrong."

"No," I said. "Everything is fine." Then I described the woman who'd taken my check.

"Yes, sir, that's me," she replied. "You must be the gentleman in the cowboy hat."

I said I was, and I told her I'd like to get to know her better if I could, maybe come back and meet her formally, and see if she would like to go out to dinner with me sometime.

She said fine, so later that week I went back to the cable office, introduced myself, and asked her to go out that night.

"Well, I'd like to," she said, "but I'm playing softball tonight." She explained that she was playing in a church league and didn't want to miss the game.

"Okay," I said, "where are you playing softball? I'll come watch."

She got a little embarrassed and started hemming and hawing because, as it turned out, she was dating someone else.

"Hey," I said, "I just want to come watch."

So she told me where she was playing, and I went over there and watched the game. After that, one thing led to another, and we started dating. That was in mid-summer, and things went so well that on Thanksgiving day, I asked her to marry me. And we got married in May of the next year—smack in the middle of that tough '81 season.

But, in a way, things worked out for the best because we got to take a honeymoon down in Cozumel right before the race in Texas, and then Junior made me unofficial car chief so I didn't have to travel with the team.

But there would be plenty of traveling later on, and, like a lot of NASCAR marriages, it was tough. During the season, I had to get to the shop early, and a lot of times, I had to stay late. Plus there was all that time on the road. But we hung in there, and we're still married, with two great kids who are almost grown. I'm glad I paid my cable bill in person that day, instead of by mail.

But back to the off-season, after that first tough year with Darrell Waltrip. I was a married man, and that changes your thinking. It's not always me, me, me. You have to start looking at things from another person's point-of-view and trying to see things the way that the other person sees them. And you have to try to figure out how to make a situation work even if it means giving a little and not getting things exactly your way. What you're looking for is results and not just the little momentary satisfaction of winning an argument or getting your way.

I'd had some experience with this kind of thinking, and I believe it helped me make the adjustments I needed to make. It happened back when I was in high school, playing football. I loved the game and wanted to play in college, but if I was going to get into college, I needed two foreign language credits.

Well, I had Spanish I from junior high, but I didn't figure I'd learned enough, and it had been a long time so I decided I wanted to repeat the course. Which I did. But unfortunately, I didn't get along with the teacher. I can be very arrogant and very stubborn, and that year I was both of those things. I wound up spending the last month of the course sitting in the hall, outside the classroom, because of my disagreements with the teacher. That's how bullheaded I was.

What that got me was four straight Fs in a class that I'd already passed back in junior high.

During the summer, I started thinking about what I'd done and how my stubbornness and pride had come back to bite me in the backside. I *still* wanted to play college football, and I *still* needed those Spanish credits. There was only one Spanish teacher in the school, and if I was going to get the credits I needed, it was going to be in her class.

I went in and talked to that teacher. I apologized and made some promises, and I assured her that I had learned something. I was able to convince her to let me go into Spanish II because I had passed the Spanish I course in junior high. When school started, I knuckled down. I did what I had to do. I passed that Spanish course—got a C—and got the credit I needed to go on to college and play football. That was the big goal, and I'd lost sight of it when I started focusing on petty things that didn't really count for much.

I feel like that was one of those experiences that helped me later on in life, especially when it came time for me to talk to Junior about how I could be crew chief and learn to deal with Darrell.

I realized that it was up to me to make the changes, and I was willing to make them. So I went in and saw Junior and used whatever credibility I had with him.

"I want to do this," I told him. "I see what needs to be done. I think, with a little help from you, I can make this thing work."

Junior listened to what I said, and he thought about it for a minute. Then he said, "Okay. Let's see if we can."

Junior Johnson never just played a hunch. He brought in two other guys—Mike Hill and Doug Richert—and set up a kind of tri-captain deal going into that season. I guess he wanted to make sure he had some backup if it turned out I couldn't get along with Darrell and things went south on him. If I started floundering, then Junior would already have those two other guys, right there, that he could go to.

But I was the go-to guy because of my seniority. I would be going to the track, and I would be the one on the radio, talking to Darrell and calling the race. When Darrell wasn't happy about something, I was the one he came to. I had to listen to his complaints, and I had to make things right or explain things to him and calm him down. It wasn't going to be an easy job, and it wasn't always going to be fun.

I was a young man, and I knew that I was on probation with both the driver and the owner of the team. I also knew we were up against some strong competition, especially from the M.C. Anderson team that was now sort of a Junior Johnson team in exile. They'd hired away our old driver, old crew chief, old engine man, and old fabricator. We felt like we *had* to beat them, to prove that Junior wasn't wrong to let them go and put his faith in us. Plus, there were some guys out there, such as Dale Earnhardt and Bobby Allison, who felt like they had a little something to prove. And, finally, we were coming off a 12-win season, which was a remarkable thing in NASCAR, so we had to measure up to our own high standards.

The pressure was on us, and we were playing way over our heads. And it was great.

It would probably be nice to say that Darrell met me halfway. But Darrell didn't change. He still wanted perfection from these cars.

And I tried to give it to him. That was my job. What I'd come to understand—in the last half of the last season and during the off-season—was that Darrell Waltrip was a different kind of driver and, maybe, a new kind of driver. But he was still a Junior Johnson kind of driver. And that means that, above all, he was a money-making driver. Darrell wanted to get as much out of the car as he possibly could.

This was something that had changed in NASCAR. The new breed of winning driver—Dale Earnhardt, Rusty Wallace, Darrell Waltrip—didn't just show up at the track and drive the car. These drivers were involved in getting the car ready to race in a way that drivers from the older generation never had been. The new drivers had to be involved because things were getting so much more competitive that little differences counted for so much. Your driver knew how the car was handling in practice, and if he could explain to you what he thought the car needed to make it go just a little faster through the turns, then you needed to listen to him and make the adjustments.

Darrell Waltrip was now a veteran driver, and he had learned some things along the way. He may not have learned how to be a diplomat or how to control that mouth of his, but he'd learned that you win races by getting the most out of your equipment. That's something that Junior had been preaching ever since I'd been with him and probably for a long time before that. It was the reason we'd been able to go that whole season without a DNF back when Cale was driving. Darrell was a believer in getting the absolute most out of the equipment, and we needed to work together to make that happen.

Where Cale believed he could carry the car, Darrell wanted the car to carry him . . . right up to the point where he needed to take over and give it that last little kick that only a great driver could give. It was a way of thinking about the equipment that had us building a lot of race cars and making a lot of changes and then, sometimes, changing things back. And it was frustrating until you saw the method in the madness, and, gradually, I began to see that and to at least understand that Darrell and Junior and I were all after the same thing—winning.

So starting in the off-season, I went to work to make it happen. I learned to listen to what Darrell was saying and not pay so much attention to how he was saying it. I suppose it was sort of like the way a movie director deals with a temperamental star. And believe me, when you sat up on the wall at pit row and watched him drive that car, you knew that Darrell Waltrip was some kind of artist. So I realized that what I needed to do was focus on the performance. Everything else—the shouting matches and the trantrums—that was just background noise. It wasn't my job to win arguments with Darrell. My job was to win races with him. I had to manage the driver the same way I managed the equipment and the rest of the crew.

But with the driver and the crew chief, I knew there has to be a special relationship. I wanted to bond with Darrell so that when I left that track, at the end of the race, I'd be just as tired as he was. That was important. If he had a complaint about the car, it was my complaint. I wanted him to feel relaxed and confident in his working space, which was the inside of the car. I wanted to be an extention of that driver. And, with time, that happened, and we got to be friends off the track. But the real relationship was when we were racing . . . and winning.

I realized how much Darrell responded to praise so when I could hear, through the headphones, that he was getting discouraged out on the track, I'd start building him up, telling him that he was running a great race, that he had 'em right where he wanted 'em, and that he just had to keep on driving and he'd be the first to the finish line. When Darrell needed to vent, I let him vent on me.

"All right, Darrell," I'd tell him. "You're right. We'll take care of it."

I tried to make things right for my driver to put him in the best possible position to win. That meant I got the equipment in the best possible shape, and I tried to get the driver's mind in the best possible shape. I wanted Darrell to believe in the equipment so that he could go out there and drive it with confidence.

That's how you win races, and I was more interested in winning races than winning arguments in the garage. Nobody remembers who won the argument; they remember who won the race.

And Darrell and I won races together, too. A lot of them. But not right away.

We felt good when we went to Daytona, which was now the first race of the year, the big kickoff to the season. We didn't have to make that long trip out to California and then back again before Speedweeks, and I think everybody was happy with that. Daytona was the big show, and we liked coming in there with everything a clean slate. But it was a little bit daunting for me that such a big race was going to be my first race as crew chief. I wasn't going to get to try out this act on the road. My first performance was going to be on the biggest stage of all.

I probably should have been eaten up with nerves back at the shop in the weeks before the race, but the truth is we were just too busy getting the car ready to race. I was focusing really hard on that and on keeping everybody—especially Darrell and Junior—in the loop. I knew that was really important.

Also, it helped me a lot to know that I had Junior there behind me. With some owners, you'd have hated having them around. You'd feel like someone was looking over your shoulder, trying to catch you in a mistake. But it wasn't that way with Junior. You knew that he was there to help you, and, buddy, if you weren't willing to listen and take help from Junior Johnson, then your ego was way too big for the job. I always felt that having Junior around gave us an edge. He'd forgotten more about racing than most of us knew.

Junior was never the kind of owner to have team meetings and do a lot of rah, rah stuff, like a football coach. But he was probably the ultimate hands-on owner, and by that I mean he was involved in everything. Junior would be there when you dynoed the engine, and if there was something he noticed, he'd tell you about it. And there were some things he wouldn't let anyone else do, like shot peen the piston rods. That was a way of stress relieving the rods that Junior thought was important and had to be done just so. He did that himself, on a machine there in the shop.

So we were all busy and all very involved in getting the car ready to go down to Daytona. I don't think it ever really hit me that I was now the crew chief and the man who was responsible for the team until we got to the track and went to get the car inspected. That's when I signed the NASCAR form certifying that the car complied with all the rules and standards. That was a big, big moment in my life. My pulse went up a little, and my mouth went dry when I took that clipboard and signed my name in the block where it said, "Crew Chief."

Yes, sir, that would be me. Mrs. Hammond's boy, Jeff, crew chief for the number 11 car, the Junior Johnson Buick.

After that, we were practicing and working on the car and running in the Busch Clash and the 125-mile Qualifier. Junior had a rule that if you were on his team, you were first to the track in the morning and last to leave at night so I was too busy to really be thinking about what a big deal this was and wondering if I was up to it. I was too deep in it for that.

I probably didn't sleep all that well the night before the race. Most crew chiefs don't. You are always thinking about what you might have forgotten to do—some little thing you could have done to give yourself that edge. I ate a good dinner, and then, for a couple of hours before I went to bed, I looked over my notes, studied the lap times, and tried to visualize the way the race would play out the next day. I pictured the cars that I thought would be our main competition and what kind of race they'd try to run. Then I thought about what we'd have to do to beat them. I ran through a couple of imaginary pit stops and tried to visualize them going clean and fast, the way we'd need for them to go if we were going to win the race. We hadn't ever done a pit stop together, as a team, in a race. The first time would be in the Daytona 500. That was a big question mark—one more thing for me to think about.

Finally, it was race day. I went to the track early and got everything arranged in the pits. I made sure we had everything we needed and that everything was where it was supposed to be. I went over the car one last time. I started in the front, and one of the other guys started in the back. We went over every square inch of the car, checking everything down to the last nut and bolt. We met in the middle and kept going so everything got checked twice.

I helped Darrell get into the car and made sure that he was buckled in and that the steering wheel was on right and locked down. Then I gave him his helmet, and when he put it on, we did a radio check. Then we shook hands, and I told him to go get 'em.

The next thing was that ritual announcement: "Gentlemen, start your engines." I'd heard it a thousand times before, but I don't believe I'd ever heard it quite the same way as I did that day. Here I was, the crew chief for the defending Winston Cup champion team, and this was the Daytona 500.

When they ran the pace lap, the roar of the crowd—150,000

strong—and the sound of the engines seemed to get right down inside of me. Right there, before they dropped the flag, it hit me what a big deal this was. But before I had a chance to get nervous or faint or anything, we were racing, and all of a sudden I got really busy.

We had a good car that day and were running out front, and Darrell was driving a good, smart race. So far, so good. Nobody had tapped me on the shoulder and told me to get off the track and quit pretending I was a crew chief. After a while it was time for the test. I told Darrell to bring it on in for our first pit stop.

Everybody in racing knows how important good stops can be, and it felt like we were on the biggest stage in the world. Three hundred thousand eyes were watching to see if we'd fall on our butts. Actually, there was only one set of eyes that I was aware of. The baby blues that belonged to Junior Johnson.

The car came rolling in and stopped, and we were over the wall and moving, everybody doing his job. Jack the car, pop the lug nuts, mount the tire, tighten the nuts, drop the car, go around the car, and do it all again. *Go, go, go.* Keep moving and get that car out of there and back on the track. Every second you waste is costing you position and money.

It felt like we were dancers, doing a routine we'd done a million times, and we pulled it off clean and fast. We knew it, and so did our driver. On his way down pit lane, getting back to the track, Darrell was hollering into the radio, "Thataway. Thataway. Great stop. Great stop, boys. That's how we need to do it."

Right then, even though it was still early in the race, I was thinking we had us a team, a car, a driver—everything we needed. We'd put all that together, and now, buddy, we might just win this race. Man, I was pumped.

Then, on the 151st lap, with Darrell running out front and clear sailing ahead, the engine blew. Our day was over and so was my chance to win the big prize in my first race as crew chief. Just like that, the air went out of my balloon. No champagne on Victory Lane. No photographs with Miss Daytona 500. Not today. Darrell brought the car in, and we loaded it up and went home.

That Daytona race was always unlucky for Darrell.

Bobby Allison won at Daytona that day, and I figured we'd be hearing from him all season long. Cale Yarborough ran second. He'd be racing a limited schedule—that was part of his deal with M.C. Anderson—but that didn't mean he wouldn't be going all out when he did race. We'd be hearing from him, too, and that team was the one we wanted to beat. So that made the DNF at Daytona that much harder to take. We were kind of down when we were loading everything up, and it felt like a long drive home. It always does when you don't win, but this one was even longer.

We were sitting on the pole the next week at Richmond, but Darrell had some bad luck and got caught up early in a wreck that wasn't his fault. We finished at the back of the pack. There was nothing any of us could have done. It was just one of those racing things. But I was still discouraged and starting to feel a little extra pressure. It was early in the season, but I was feeling like the driver—I think it was Buddy Baker—who was in a slump and told people he was going down to the grocery store to buy a stalk of bananas for the monkey who was riding around on his back. I wanted to get that first win. The whole team did.

If we couldn't get the win at Daytona in the 500, then the place where I'd want to get it would be Bristol. Of all the tracks on the circuit, that's the one where I would pay money to sit in any seat and watch a race. Bristol is the roots of NASCAR, the pure thing. It's short track racing in a big arena. The track is ½ mile with some of the

highest banking anywhere so they run really fast. They've kept building onto the stands so now they can put more than 150,000 people in there. It has the flavor of the old Roman Coliseum and the Rose Bowl, both.

The racing at Bristol is hard-charging, paint-swapping, fender-banging, old-style NASCAR when everybody had learned how to do it on dirt tracks, and you didn't have power steering and a specially designed air-conditioning system to keep the drivers from passing out in the heat. What you had at Bristol was part race and part fight.

You fought the car and the track and the other drivers, and your endurance and your stamina counted for as much as your equipment. There are more relief drivers used at Bristol, by far, than at any other track. Drivers just get worn down by the g-forces and the hard racing. You can't ever let up, and you can't ever relax. There aren't any long straightaways where you can just let it go. You've got to be on top of the car, driving it, all the time. If you aren't, you'll be side-ways, or upside down, in a heartbeat.

Racing at Bristol is more competitive than it is at any other track. There is a lot of passing and, like I say, a lot of beating and banging. There are more driver and crew altercations there than anywhere else. You know when you go there that there is a good chance you'll be in a fight as well as a race.

There are two races every season at Bristol. Since 1976, three dri-vers had won all the races there—Cale Yarborough, Dale Earnhardt, and Darrell Waltrip. Cale won four straight there and did it by just going out and wrestling that track to the ground. Everybody knows how Earnhardt drove, and his "Intimidator" style worked really well at Bristol. He'd put on the helmet, pull up the gloves, and get after it. He figured to be the last man standing—or running, as the case may be. Darrell Waltrip was a little different, and if you didn't really know racing that well, you wouldn't figure him for a driver who'd do well at Bristol.

But Darrell could fool you that way. He was so smooth that you thought of him as purely a finesse driver. But the truth is Darrell was a *complete* driver. And he was a smart driver. He knew that on a track where everyone is wrecking, the best way to win a race might be to find the holes and get through them without hitting anyone—or getting hit. Darrell knew what Junior was always saying—that the car runs better when you don't wreck it. That was something that Dale Earnhardt was still learning.

Darrell didn't back off—unless he could do so and make it work for him and use it to win the race. Earnhardt didn't back off even if it meant he'd get knocked off the track and out of the race. It might have made him "the Intimidator," but in those early years, it also made him one of those drivers who had "DNF" written after his name in a lot of races.

I was excited when we went up to Bristol for the third race of the season. I loved the track and the race, and I knew I had a driver who could win there because he'd done it before. A Junior Johnson car had won 14 races out of the last 21 at Bristol, and you had to like those odds. But I was also nervous because it seemed like we were running a streak of bad luck and if there is any track in the world that can reach out and bite you and take you right out of a race, then it is Bristol.

Things got off to a good start. Darrell won the pole. That doesn't mean as much at a short track, but you like to get out front early in the race and let the first big wrecks happen behind you. That's a lot easier than coming up on a wreck from behind and having to pick your way through it. So we liked sitting on the pole. It meant we had a fast car, and we might not have to play dodgeball for the first 100 laps or so.

Darrell ran a smart race. He stayed up close, and somewhere around the 400th lap he was running second by about 10 seconds. Then the leader, Earnhardt, got into it with another car. Darrell saw an opportunity, and he took it. He cruised right by 'em into the lead and never looked back. He crossed the finish line about 13 seconds in front of Earnhardt, and we had our first win of the season—my first win as crew chief.

It might have been one of the happiest moments of my life, standing there in Victory Lane. I know, for sure, that I'd never felt such a sense of relief. I hadn't realized how much pressure I was under to win—until I won. With the pressure off, all of a sudden, I could feel what a load I'd been carrying around.

So we celebrated, and I soaked up the cheering and the champagne. It was just as fine as I'd dreamed it would be. You hear about people struggling for something, working hard to reach some sort of goal, and when they get there, they have the feeling of, "Is that all there is?"

Not me. Not for a minute.

I was one of the other kind of people. Once I'd gotten what I'd been working so hard for, what I wanted was more. I had always wanted to succeed and to win, and I had been wanting to win at racing since I was 12 years old. All these years now, it had been my life, and here I was at the top of the racing world.

There are people who look at NASCAR racing and wonder how you can do it, week after week. Year after year. You go to the same tracks, and you run around in circles. They wonder, "Doesn't it get *old*. Don't you ever feel like you've had enough of left-hand turns?"

What I tell 'em is, "Nope. Not ever in the 500 races I started as crew chief."

The thing is, every race is different. Even if you've run on the same track before, it's different when you come back the next time. Ask a driver if running around in circles, lap after lap, doesn't get to be boring, and what he'll tell you is, "Every lap is different. The car handles just a little different each time because the tires are warmer and you're carrying less fuel and the surface of the track is slicker. Conditions are always changing, and you're constantly trying to stay on top of them."

In racing, nothing ever stays the same, and you win by thinking and adjusting and being quick. If you get bored or tired or slow, then you lose, or worse.

When you stand out there before a race, and you hear the cheering of 150,000 people, and you know that millions of other people are watching on television . . . well, you just can't imagine the pump. It is something you can't get enough of. I used to tell people that when the day came that I could hear the words "Gentlemen, start your engines" and *not* get goose bumps, that was the day I was going to walk away.

It hasn't happened yet. I'm broadcasting now, instead of crew chiefing, but I still feel that way. Still get those goose bumps.

Racing gets into your blood, like football gets into some people. They just love the feeling and smell and the sensation of walking into a locker room before a game or a practice. I get that same thing when I walk onto pit row and smell the engine oil, gasoline, and rubber and hear the sound of engines running.

When I left Victory Lane at Bristol that April day, there was just one thought on my mind. Getting back.

And, in fact, we won again the very next week in Atlanta. We beat Richard Petty by 2 inches. Literally. It was one of the closest races I'd ever seen. Cale Yarborough ran third, making the win that much sweeter. We'd won on a short track and a superspeedway now, so we knew how to get it done. The trick was going to be to keep on doing it. Just that simple—and that hard.

In the early part of the season, we seemed to be getting into a habit of winning or wrecking. At Rockingham, somebody had a water hose break, and several cars, including Darrell's, went sliding into the wall. "It was like ice out there," he said.

We got the car back on the track, and Darrell limped in at seventh place.

We crashed again, the next week, at Darlington and couldn't finish.

Then we kept it in one piece at North Wilkesboro and won the race. We'd won three races now, but Terry Labonte and Benny Parsons were leading in the points and neither of them had won anything.

"Just keep winning races," Junior always told us, "and the points will take care of themselves.

We didn't win at Martinsville, where we had to swap out engines in the car right before the race, but we ran good enough to get up to second in the points by coming in fifth. Darrell always had a sense of humor about these things. "Routine day," he said after that race. "Changed motors, blew two tires, hit two walls, and spun out. Strictly routine."

We went down to Talladega for the spring race there, and the cars were *fast*. That is a 2½-mile track with the highest banking in NASCAR, and teams were laying down some really blistering qualifying laps. Benny Parsons had a car that his crew chief, Waddell Wilson, had set up to run at superspeedways. It went so fast it just about pulled the paint right off the sheet metal. Parsons wound up taking the pole, and his qualifying speed was more than 200 mph. That was the first time anyone had ever done that.

Benny ran out front a lot in that fast car, but there were plenty of other drivers who were in it. The lead kept going back and forth—I believe it changed something like 50 times—and on the last lap, Parsons was ahead with three other drivers close. Benny went down low to block a slingshot, and then, out of nowhere, here came Darrell, with Labonte drafting him. I mean, they were coming on *hard*. Just eating up the track.

Right there at the end, Darrell got around Benny and won the race. Labonte came in second. Later on, I watched a replay of the television broadcast. Ken Squier, who was announcing, was saying, "Looks like Parsons has this one . . . *hold everything, here comes Waltrip.*"

It was one of the most exciting races I'd ever been involved in, and it was even more exciting watching the replay and listening to Squier, turned my knuckles white.

We left Talladega with four wins. But we were still second in the points to Labonte.

"Just win races," Junior kept saying, and we kept doing it. We won the next week, too, at Nashville. We'd won half the races that season. Nobody else was close. Certainly not Labonte, who hadn't won any but was still leading in the points.

We blew an engine at Dover and another one the next week at Charlotte. The fans cheered when Darrell spun out at Charlotte. He might have been the winningest driver in NASCAR, but he was still the least popular. We were doing everything we could to change his image and get the fans to like him. We'd walk around the track before a race, giving out sponsor hats. They had the Mountain Dew colors and Darrell's name and car number on them. I don't know if many people ever wore those hats because nothing we tried seemed to turn it around for Darrell. The fans were really down on him.

And Darrell, being an emotional guy, didn't like it. After they cheered him for blowing an engine and spinning out at Charlotte that day, Darrell was being interviewed and he said he wanted those fans "to meet me in the Kmart parking lot and we'll duke it out."

He was hot.

We saw that side of Darrell again a couple of races later up in Michigan. He was running close behind Cale Yarborough for the last 30 or 40 laps. Junior—who didn't want to beat anyone in racing as much as he wanted to beat Cale and that M.C. Anderson team—got on the radio and said to Darrell, "Boy, don't you let him beat you."

Well, that was like the voice of the Almighty.

Darrell worked the car a little harder and squeezed out a lead on the last lap. They were running really close in the third turn, and when they touched doors, Cale came out of it ahead and held on to get the win.

Darrell was so mad about losing the race—and losing it to Cale—that on the cool-down lap he came racing up behind Yarborough's car like he was going to ram him.

"I wanted to run him clean off the race track," Darrell told me later. "Then at the last minute, I realized I couldn't do that."

So he tried to back off and when he did, he spun the car out and wound up stuck in the mud in the infield. Cale said something about how maybe they needed to meet in the Kmart parking lot to settle it.

Very embarrassing. Worse, we were losing ground to Labonte and Bobby Allison, who won the next week to take the points lead.

We were racing for the championship against Allison, who we'd beaten the year before and who had a history with Junior. Allison was one of the great drivers in the history of NASCAR, no doubt about it. But he hadn't won the championship when he was with Junior, back in the early '70s, and they hadn't parted on the best of terms. Even more than most drivers, he didn't like getting beat by Junior Johnson teams. When we won, Allison figured it was because we were cheating.

Well, now he was in a close race for the Cup with us, and it was getting to him, the same way that Richard Petty had gotten to

Darrell a couple of years earlier. We were behind, but we were closing. Allison could see the number 11 car in his mirror, and it made him nervous.

We won the Talladega 500 in August. That made Darrell the first ever two-time winner of that race. And it was the second time we'd won on that track in this season. Usually, you are happy to just survive a couple of races at Talladega. Everybody runs so fast there, and usually so tightly packed, that any small wreck becomes a big wreck really quickly. Talladega is where people are always worrying about "the big one."

We won again at Bristol in late August. Man, we *owned* that track. We beat Allison by less than a second, and Bobby was getting frustrated now that we were coming into the homestretch of the season. We'd be at Darlington the next week for the Labor Day race. That track is another one where you can get in trouble in a heartbeat. Darrell had lost a lot of ground there to Richard Petty when they were in that tight points race in 1979. Darrell was ahead in the points, but he could see Petty coming up behind him. He was trying too hard, and he hit the wall twice at Darlington. It was one of those deals where he knew he had to be cool and race smart, but he was young and hadn't ever won a championship. He wanted it so badly that he let his emotions get away from him.

Darrell was a different driver now. He'd won a championship, and he drove with a lot more . . . maybe *cunning* is the word. He drove like Junior would have if he'd still been racing. Darrell drove to win—he didn't stroke it—but he drove with his brains as well as his right foot and his two hands.

Still I knew we had to be careful at Darlington, where the least little mistake can cost you. We were running behind in the points, and Darrell might get overeager.

Allison, who we figured was the main competition, ran out front until he cut a tire just short of 100 laps. He lost a lot of time and didn't figure to be a factor. Then Labonte, who was just ahead of us, at second place in the points, blew an engine on lap 120. Darrell was running a good, smart race, keeping the car on the track and running in second place until we blew an engine on lap 240.

So instead of closing some ground on Allison at Darlington, we dropped a little farther back. But we weren't out of it, and we weren't quitting. In a funny way, we left Darlington even more confident that we were going to get that second straight points championship. We weren't cocky, or anything like that, but we did feel like we had a good team, a good car, and a good driver. We'd won more races than anyone else, and we'd probably win some more. The points, like Junior always said, would take care of themselves.

The points took care of themselves, all right, but the winner of the next race, at Richmond, was Allison, and now he was stretching it out. It was Allison's first short track win in more than 2 years, so it seemed like he had the momentum. He was up more than 140 points with just seven races left. We'd run third and lost ground. But we still weren't quitting.

We went up to Dover needing to win. We were running out of time, and Allison's taillights were getting dimmer and dimmer with him pulling away from us. So we sucked it up, and Darrell ran down Kyle Petty and Bill Elliott to win the race. Allison had a water leak, and it was all he could do to finish the race. We cut his lead by more than a third, down to just over 100 points.

We knew we had to just keep winning races.

North Wilkesboro was next on the dance card, and Darrell won there, too. He and Bobby were racing in the early going, trading the lead back and forth, and then Bobby blew an engine. You could feel the frustration coming off his crew down pit lane when he brought it in. And if the crew was frustrated, then things were really getting to Bobby. He'd been racing for a long time, gone through a lot of cars and owners, been an owner himself, and won plenty of races. But he'd never taken that last step to the championship. And there wasn't any secret about how badly he wanted it. Truth is, Bobby might have been putting too much pressure on himself and his team.

That team, by the way, was the DiGard operation. Allison was driving the number 88 Gatorade car that had been Waltrip's ride before he came over to Junior. You knew that those boys over there wanted to beat us worse than anyone on the track. We wanted to beat them back, and even though he was running behind, Darrell was saying things to kind of get inside their heads. He knew how much pressure they were under, and he remembered how it had been in '79 when Petty ran him down. So Darrell knew from the other side how the challenger can play loose and drive, and that's what he was doing to Allison. We were the confident, loose team even though we were still behind, even after the win at North Wilkesboro.

But it was close. Just 15 points. We figured to take it all the way down to the wire.

We lost ground the next week at Charlotte. But in a way Allison came out of the race in worse shape than we did—psychologically, anyway. He lead the race for almost 300 laps and was out front with 10 laps to go when he blew an engine and finished ninth. Darrell had gotten tangled up in a wreck earlier so he got a 14th. We dropped back to 37 points behind Allison, but you just knew he and his team felt like they'd blown it on a race they should have won. To come that close—10 laps—and lose it on a mechanical problem, you have to believe you are jinxed and that it's just not meant to happen. Instead of thinking about how you're going to win this thing, you start pointing fingers, accusing other teams of cheating, and thinking, "what's next."

I'd say that leaving Charlotte we felt like we had 'em right where we wanted 'em.

Sure enough, we won at Martinsville the next week, and Allison blew another engine. It was the third race in a row that had happened to him. He'd been leading the race for almost 100 laps when it did. It was almost enough to make you feel sorry for those boys. *Almost.* But we knew we wouldn't have gotten any sympathy from them if it had been the other way around. Like I said, this rivalry wasn't exactly friendly.

Anyway, we were celebrating. We had the win, and we were ahead in the points. The win was particularly sweet because it was number 50 for Darrell, and that tied him on the all-time list with Junior Johnson.

Darrell went ahead of Junior the next week at Rockingham. This was one win that didn't do much for us in the points. Allison got so many lap points that we came out of the race exactly where we started—37 points ahead. But we weren't complaining.

Allison was, though. He was leading the race when he came in for his final pit stop. The crew did a great job and got him out in 12.7 seconds, which is a great time, and that should have sewed it up if the engine held up and the car didn't wreck.

Well, probably because he was feeling the pressure and wanted that championship so badly, Allison pushed a little too hard and spun out on the first turn coming out of the pits. Darrell went by him and won the race by about 10 seconds.

"We had it won," Allison said, later on. "Best car, best engine, best everything. Then I spun off pit road and lost it."

But Allison was a warrior. He won the next week in Atlanta. It came down to the last 10 laps after a caution, and Allison beat us out of the pits. It was really close at the end, and it closed up the points race, too. We now led by 22 with one race to go, at Riverside.

We went out to California feeling confident. The DiGard team, even after the Atlanta race, was pressing. The mood over there wasn't good, and things got to the point where in the garage at Riverside one day Junior came in and found Davey Allison—Bobby's son—snooping around our car with a magnet. He was trying to find out if we had any illegal aluminum on the car, instead of sheet metal, so we could shave a few pounds of weight. That's how bad things had gotten.

Davey was a teenager then, just a kid. So Junior threw him out of the garage and told NASCAR to get the word over to the DiGard people that the next time it happened, he wasn't going to be so nice about it.

Bad luck—or something—bit Allison again in the race. He needed a big finish, and he sure didn't get it. First, he had tires go flat, and then he had some problems with his lug nuts. Finally, late in the race, he blew another engine.

Darrell went out to Riverside knowing that he had to run a smart, conservative race, and that's what he did. But he was still an excitable driver, and on one turn, he missed a shift and thought the transmission had gone bad on him.

"Get a gear box, get a gear box," he hollered into the radio. "I can't shift it."

So I got on the radio and calmed him down. "Take it easy, DW," I said. "Take it easy. Try it again."

Darrell settled down and figured out that he'd lost third gear, but he could still drive it.

And Darrell drove a good race. Took third on a road course, and I think that was just more proof of what a complete driver he'd become. That year, he won those two at Talladega so there wasn't any question he could drive the big tracks. He won on the short tracks at

Bristol and North Wilkesboro. And he probably could have won at Riverside, on the road course, if he hadn't been playing safe and nursing that transmission. He won other road races in his career. He'd made himself into the whole package.

We won the Cup by 72 points, and that night we celebrated.

Winning a NASCAR race is hard. A million different things can happen to cost you a win. You can have some little $10 part break on the last lap; you can get caught up in a wreck that somebody else started; you might have a great car and just get behind one that is faster that day. People in racing don't always accept that another car is faster or that another team did a better job. These are

supremely competitive people who don't like losing, and occasionally they can have a hard time admitting that they got beat fair and square.

There aren't too many races where some driver doesn't think another driver cut him off or wrecked him on purpose. You hear it all the time, and sometimes it is even true. Drivers want to win, and they'll push the rules to do it. There is a fine line between racing hard and racing dirty, and there have been drivers who made a living out of walking that line. Dale Earnhardt comes to mind right away. And among the current crop of drivers, you've got Tony Stewart, Jimmy Spencer, and Kurt Busch. They'll all get into you, the way that Earnhardt did, and other drivers will claim they lost races because these guys used dirty tactics.

When you can't blame another driver, you can always say that he had a car that wasn't legal. That is an old, reliable standby that has been around as long as NASCAR. Right from the start, they called it "stock car racing" because it was supposed to be between off-the-shelf cars, the kind anyone could go out and buy. In the earliest days of NASCAR, people were racing the family car, the same one they'd used to drive to the grocery store. That changed pretty quickly, but the rules still called for stock cars.

Naturally, people worked on them to make them go faster and handle better. Like I said before, the thinking was if there wasn't a rule against it, you went ahead and did it. NASCAR was always having to rewrite and expand the rule book to make sure nobody had an unfair advantage, but it was a constant struggle between the ingenuity of the people working on the cars and the thoroughness of the people writing the rules.

The quest to find little creases in the rules was one thing that everyone understood and could live with. If you were smart enough to find some little thing that NASCAR had overlooked and take advantage of it then, hey, good for you. Junior Johnson had always been the master of this sort of thing.

But there has always been a certain amount of outright cheating, too. For instance, the cars have always had to be of certain dimensions: this long, this high, this wide, this far off the ground, and so forth. Obviously, if you could find a way to get around those limits and make a smaller, lower, narrower car, then you would have an advantage. And sure enough, once in the early days, a driver showed up at some race with a car that was faster than anything on the track. It was just passing everybody. But there was something about that car that just didn't *look* right to the other drivers and crews. Finally, somebody got out a tape and measured that car. It had been built about 3 percent smaller than the stock dimensions. It was not enough to be really obvious but enough to give it an advantage.

So NASCAR started building templates that they would fit over every car in the pre-race inspections.

But that didn't stop people from looking for ways to cheat. Some guys ran big engines—more cubic inches of displacement than the rules allowed. You could catch that in inspections, but that didn't stop people from trying it. You could look for ways to carry extra fuel so you could stay out on the track longer than the other cars, especially at the end, when they were having to pit for extra fuel to finish the race. Guys came up with some pretty ingenious ways of carrying extra fuel. Gary Nelson, who was Bobby Allison's crew chief in the years we were competing so hard with them, came up with a system for carrying extra fuel in what we called the "package tray." That was the area just under the rear glass, in the body of the car. For a while, they had pretty good luck.

There was also a time when guys were getting a little extra power boost from nitrous oxide. You could shoot a little laughing gas into the cylinder head, and it would give you some extra rpm. The trick was to hide the bottle and the extra lines in the car somewhere so they didn't find them in the teardown inspections. Once NASCAR caught onto this one, it got harder and harder to do, and guys who were spotted got hit with heavy fines and suspensions. So you saw less of that, which is the way it goes.

Then you had some people trying illegal additives in the fuel. So NASCAR started testing fuel. The thing is, some people will always do something illegal if they think it gives them an advantage and they aren't likely to get caught. When they start getting nailed, then they quit doing it. But that doesn't mean they don't start looking to try something else.

It's an ongoing thing, and you'd be surprised—or maybe not—at how creative people can be when it comes to looking for that little, tiny advantage. I remember one time, back while Cale Yarborough was still driving for Junior, when the crew was still over the wall after a pit stop. Who should come by me but Darrell Waltrip, who was still driving for DiGard at the time. When he went by, it felt like somebody had gone after my legs with a shotgun. They'd stuck lead bird shot up in the jack stob and then when the car was on the track, Darrell could pull a bolt and release the shot to make the car lighter. The stuff was everywhere on the track, but there wasn't anything we could do about it because NASCAR weighed the cars only before the race, not after.

In those days, you didn't necessarily go crying to NASCAR if you thought someone was cheating. You found out what they were doing and then figured out a way to do it better. So Junior decided that if they were going to play that game, he'd just go out and get himself some heavy wheels. We'd put them on for the pre-race inspection when they weighed the car. Then, during a pit stop when we were racing, we'd take those heavy wheels off and put some lighter ones on. That worked for a long time, until NASCAR started weighing cars after the race, too.

During my career as a crew chief, I got my hand slapped a couple of time by NASCAR, but I never got in a lot of trouble and never had to forfeit any points. I only received cash fines, usually on overweight issues. One time we put in a tungsten radio that was about 10 times heavier than the authorized radio. It put some extra weight over the outside tires to make the car stick better to the track. We got caught on that one.

I'd have to say that there is probably less of that going on now than there was when I was in racing. The gray area has really shrunk. With the way NASCAR has gotten so strict, the boys today are getting the death penalty for things that would have gotten us a speeding ticket. For example, Richard Petty won his 200th race in the season I'm getting ready to tell you about in a car that wouldn't have made it onto the racetrack today. It's gotten too risky to do some of those things. But that isn't to say some of it doesn't still go on.

The long and the short of it is there is always going to be cheating. It is easy to accuse someone, harder to prove. And it is usually the losing teams accusing the winners of cheating. For this reason, Junior seemed to attract a fair number of those kind of complaints. In a way, it was a compliment. The people making those accusations weren't just scapegoating. They were acknowledging what everyone knew—that Junior was maybe one of the shrewdest people in NASCAR when it came to cars, rules, going fast, and winning races.

And, the truth is, Junior had been caught once or twice. There was a time, before I went to work for him, when Junior's team had been caught running a car with a big engine. And Bobby Allison had once driven for Junior. So it was understandable when, in the heat of that '82 points race, Allison made some insinuations, like maybe we weren't winning those 12 races—and eventually that points championship—entirely on the level.

But the cheating charges in 1982 were nothing compared to 1983, when things really hit the fan.

But let's start at the beginning with Daytona. It was a race I'll never forget and one I'd never want to go through again. Not only did we not win the race; for a couple of terrible minutes there, I thought we'd lost our driver.

We had a good car, and we were all pretty optimistic when we went down to Daytona. We seemed to have bad luck there in the past, but we were hoping we'd put that behind us. And Darrell wanted to beat what was shaping up to be a jinx, so he just poured it on to get back on the lead lap when a caution came out early after Earnhardt blew an engine. Darrell wanted to beat the leader back to the flag and would have done it if the car he was coming up behind hadn't backed off at the last minute. Darrell swerved down low to get by him and lost it on a patch of grass just before the turn into pit row. He spun, real quick, and hit the inside wall *hard*. Then the car went shooting back across the track and hit the outside wall.

This all happened on turn four, and I lost sight of the car when it went down off the track and hit the inside wall. But I saw it come shooting back across the track and hit the outside wall, and I knew it was bad. The car was mangled, and from the way it came up the track, I knew that Darrell had hit hard.

I called to him on the radio a couple of times. When he didn't answer, and I didn't see any medical personnel going to the car, I took off my headphones and started running. I guess I was the first to get to the car, and I looked in the passenger side window. From the way Darrell's head was hanging, I was afraid he had broken his neck and was dead. This sick feeling just came over me.

"Darrell!" I called to him.

Nothing.

I called again. Then a couple of more times. And I was looking around for the medical people who had finally gotten there. About that time, Darrell started moving a little and making soft, kind of moaning sounds.

I knew he was alive. So I started talking to him and telling him he was all right and that we were going to take care of him. Stuff like that. I was so relieved.

But we still didn't know how badly Darrell was hurt, and we told him we were going to put a cervical collar on him so we could take him out of the car through the window. He started trying to fight us on that.

Same old Darrell. I fought back and told him that he had to do it. After a while, he let us put the collar on, and we moved him and had him on the stretcher on the ground, ready to load him into the ambulance.

About that time, the truck came by putting Speedy Dry on the track to soak up the oil that had spilled from Darrell's car. Some of the Speedy Dry got on Darrell's face, and he said, "I know why I crashed, Jeff. It was because of the rain. The track was wet, and I took a skid. It was the rain that did it."

Even half out of his head, Darrell was looking for a reason for why the crash wasn't his fault.

"Yeah, Darrell," I said. "It was the rain."

It hadn't rained at Daytona all day long.

Darrell went to the hospital. They said he had a concussion, which wasn't any surprise. They released him the next day, and he raced the next week. But he wasn't the same driver for the whole first half of the season. I didn't know it then—not for sure, anyway, but something wasn't right. Darrell didn't tell anyone just how out of it he was until much later. But he was having dizzy spells and partial amnesia and was just generally out of it for most of the spring. I think that has to be a big reason why we started so slowly that year.

Darrell never asked for a relief driver. He ran 150 laps at Richmond the next week before the gear box gave out. Later on, he told me that he didn't remember a thing about that race.

Bobby Allison won that day, and I think it became clearer and clearer as the season went on that NASCAR, the veteran drivers, and the fans did not want Darrell Waltrip to win a third straight NASCAR points championship. Darrell still wasn't a very popular driver in the first place. Cale Yarborough was one of the most popular drivers in the history of NASCAR, and he was the only one to win three straight, so people didn't want their hero's record tied by anyone, and especially not by Darrell. And then, Bobby Allison had been around a long time, and even though the Allisons could be arrogant, they had a following. Bobby was an old veteran driver who had never won a championship. He'd been sort of outdueled in his feud with Petty, and then he had come up short against Waltrip two straight seasons.

I think you'd have to say he was the sentimental favorite.

Not with us, though. We were going after that third straight championship. We didn't get our first win until the sixth race of the season, at North Wilkesboro, where we beat Allison. Then we won again the next week at Martinsville, and it felt like we had gotten it gathered up and were back in the hunt.

We crashed at Talladega and lost some ground, but we won again the next week at Nashville, making it three straight on the short tracks. Allison kind of implied we were cheating.

"He's got too much of something," Allison said about Darrell. "No one can beat him on the short tracks with that setup. A lot of us would like to know what it is."

He may have been talking about the way we set up the rear springs—outside hard, inside soft. It was something that Darrell liked and that he thought helped him get around better on short tracks. Nothing illegal about it. But when Allison won at Dover the next week, he said it was because his crew chief had been talking to one of our boys and learned something.

When someone asked the crew chief, Gary Nelson, what it was, he said, "No comment."

"NASCAR calls it being competitive," Allison said. "I don't blame Junior, but I'd like to see more integrity from the sanctioning body."

I say he was just blowing smoke. Blame Junior for *what*? Allison was leading in the points, but he could see Darrell coming up behind him, just like he had the last two seasons, and Allison was looking for a way to distract us.

By mid-June, we were up to second place in the points, less than 200 behind.

We might have won the Talladega 500 except that Allison, who was down a lap, got in Darrell's way and kept him from trying to pass Earnhardt, who beat us by 4 car lengths.

"Bobby won the race for Dale," Darrell said. "No question."

He was hot.

Earnhardt sort of agreed.

Allison wasn't making any apologies. "I thought Earnhardt could have passed Waltrip any time he wanted to," he said.

Allison was having the same kind of problems he always had. Blew an engine early at Michigan. Only seven cars got a DNF in that race, and his was one of them. When you're trying to win a championship and you look around and see that, oh, Jody Ridley is finishing and you aren't, it has to be discouraging, and it has to cause problems on a team. Especially when things like that have been happening for 3 years in a row.

We got another win at Bristol, and this one was especially gratifying to me because we got it in the pits. Darrell had been racing Earnhardt close but couldn't get around him. Both cars came in to take four tires when the yellow came out late in the race. We made a perfect stop, everything just right, and got back on the track before Earnhardt. The race got held up for rain, and while we were waiting to see if it would clear enough for us to race again, Earnhardt came over to our trailer.

"I had the race," he kept saying. "Had the race. Had the car. You won it in the pits."

NASCAR eventually called it, and we got the win. There wasn't any question that this one belonged to the crew. Dale Earnhardt, himself, said so.

We'd closed in on Allison and were just 41 points behind him. We felt like we were on a roll.

Then Allison and the DiGard team pulled it together and won three in a row.

We came back and beat Allison at North Wilkesboro. Darrell passed him with about 20 laps to go and got back some points. He was still optimistic.

"We got to make 'em race," Darrell said. Everybody thought that would be the news, from then until the end of the season, Darrell and Bobby racing for the championship. Then we had a little dust up in Charlotte that drew everybody's attention away from the points race. It was NASCAR's biggest cheating scandal ever, involving NASCAR's most famous driver ever.

We thought we had a winning car going into the October race at Charlotte. If we won, we'd pick up some more points on Allison and . . . well, who knew? We were still in this thing, and like Junior always said, "You just need to keep winning races."

And we were winning Charlotte. Had been all day long. We plainly had the strongest car. With around 20 laps to go, I thought we had it in the bag. Then here comes Richard Petty.

Now the famous 43 car hadn't done much all year, and it started this race way back—20th or something—and hadn't led a single lap all day. But suddenly it started coming on so strong that it looked like everyone else was going backward.

"Watch out for Richard," I said to Darrell over the radio.

"I'm watching," he said, "but there ain't nothing I can do."

Petty caught Darrell, passed him, and won the race by 3 seconds. Darrell brought the car into the pits, and we took it back to the garage and started loading it up to go home. We were disappointed, but we figured we'd just been beat by a better car. Petty had won a lot of races—this was the 198th of his career—so there wasn't any shame in losing to him. That's racing.

But it turned out that when Petty got through celebrating in

Victory Lane and went to the post-race teardown inspection, the first thing they found was that he was running four left-side tires. That's illegal because while it makes you run faster, it is unsafe. Another driver, Tim Richmond, had been caught doing the same thing during a previous race and was penalized 5 laps.

The race was over, so it was going to be hard to take 5 laps away from Petty. If they had, though, we would have won the race.

But the tire thing was just the beginning. You could claim that you made a mistake in the heat of the battle when you were mounting the tires and accidentally put on four lefts. I mean, it could happen.

But it isn't likely that you'd just inadvertently run an engine that exceeded the displacement limit by almost 30 cubic inches. But that's what they found under Petty's hood. We were all limited to 358 cubic inches of displacement, and he was running a mill that went almost 382.

Big problems. Lots of discussions among the NASCAR people. And all that time, nobody said anything to us. So we finished loading up, and we got out of there. And once we were out of the garage area and had left the track, that was it. NASCAR no longer had custody of the car, and they couldn't call us into the inspection area, verify that we'd been running a legal machine, and then disqualify Petty and give us the win.

That would have been the right thing to do. But Richard Petty—with NASCAR's help—stole a win from us when it still might have made a difference in the points race. What they did, instead, was take the 104 Winston Cup points away from Richard and fine him $35,000.

Richard claimed he didn't know anything about the tires or the engine.

"I just drive the car," he said.

Right. And the owner was Petty Enterprises, out of Level Cross,

North Carolina, which has been running NASCAR longer than anyone could remember.

I still get mad thinking about it. And I was a lot madder then.

But you have to get over it. If you're going to compete in this sport, you have to learn something really early about NASCAR—it is their bat and their ball and their field. If you are lucky, they'll let you wear the uniform. It is what it is.

Are they manipulative? Yes.

Are they controlling? Yes.

Do they intentionally screw over the individual? No.

We all step into this thing with our eyes wide open, and we learn really early that when NASCAR makes a decision—whether it's about the number of square inches they'll allow on a spoiler or what to do about Richard Petty when they catch him cheating—they will do what they consider to be "in the best interests of the sport." It was in the best interest of the sport, that day, for Petty to get the win even though we deserved it and had earned it.

You learn to live with it. Even if you don't like it much.

I don't know how much the mess at Charlotte affected our performance the rest of the year. When it gets down to it, you either win or you make excuses. We didn't win, but I don't like making excuses. So let's just say this—we didn't get it done.

Darrell ran good enough in the two races after Charlotte to be 64 points down going into the last race of the season at Riverside. We thought we had a chance when Bobby Allison cut a tire early in the race. But he kept racing and got back on the lead lap.

Allison had six wins for the season and so did we. But he beat us for the championship by 47 points. It was one of those where you think about the "what ifs."

There was the wreck at Daytona that got us off to a bad start. Then the loss at Talladega when Allison blocked us. Then the Petty race at

Charlotte. And a lot of other little things along the way that added up.

It was disappointing. I didn't feel like we'd finished in second place. I figured we'd lost. And I wanted for the off-season to be over with so we could come back and do it again.

*T*he big change, coming into the 1984 season, was that Junior Johnson was going to be running two teams. He had a new partner named Warner Hodgdon, who was one of those guys who gets into racing after he's made a lot of money in something else. They get into racing for the glamor. It's the same way you see people buy football teams or baseball teams after they've gotten rich in insurance or ship-

building or something. Most of these people are the straight goods, but sometimes the empire that is behind all the money is a little shaky. That's the way it was with Hodgdon, who eventually had to declare bankruptcy. He claimed he lost $50 million because of something some crooked employee did. That seemed like kind of a reach, but by then, Junior and everyone else in racing had cut loose from him.

Still, we didn't know any of this when Junior signed up Neil Bonnett to drive the other car and put Doug Richert over there as crew chief. Of course, you see multiple team operations all over NASCAR these days, but back then running even two teams was unorthodox and—the way some people saw it—downright radical. But Junior was never one to stand still for very long. He was always innovating, and he was ready to try the two team setup.

The rest of us didn't have any say in the matter, and we just went along with it. We'd done all right, up to now, following Junior's lead. If any of us did have reservations, they weren't very strong, and nobody was talking about them.

In the first race of the year, it looked like maybe things were going to work out. We didn't win Daytona—the jinx held—but we finished third. Neil Bonnett, driving Junior's other car, finished right behind us in fourth. That was the good news.

The bad news was we lost the race to Cale Yarborough. That would have been bad enough, all by itself. What made it worse is how Cale beat us. Late in the race, he tucked in behind Darrell Waltrip, who was leading, and just hung on his bumper, drafting around the track with him until the last lap when he slingshoted him and won the race. The last-lap pass is sort of like a 15th-round knockout or a 9th-inning, bases-loaded strikeout. It is one of those things in sports that cuts the heart out of your opponent. Cale's last six wins had come on last-lap passes. He was just about the toughest, cagiest old veteran out there, and I think that pass might have proved to Darrell and me that even though we had won a couple of championships, there were still some things we could learn.

That's not saying that there was any shame in losing to Cale Yarborough, especially not in a race where he'd won the pole, which he had. Still, those last-lap passes do hurt.

After Daytona, we staggered through the spring. Got a second at Richmond, then got docked five positions for an illegal pass at Atlanta. We were like an engine that is running a little rough. We stayed close in the points, but we weren't where we thought we should be. Then we got everything sorted out and won at Bristol on April Fool's Day. This was the seventh straight race Darrell had won on that track. To my way of thinking, that just about says it all, right there, about Darrell Waltrip. Bristol is a driver's track; it's one of the two or three toughest on the whole NASCAR circuit. You don't win there by just steering; you've got to *drive*.

We left Bristol ahead in the points. It was only a 5-point lead, but we figured we were back in shape.

We were convinced of it when Darrell won at Darlington, NASCAR's other notorious track, a couple of weeks later. It was one of those bumper-car days there at Darlington, and 25 of the 38 cars had at least some body damage when the race was over. Some of those had a *lot* of damage. Darrell's car was in fine shape. He'd waited for all the crashing to be over, and then he went out front and led the race for 117 of the last 118 laps.

We were cooking now, but the Bonnett team was having problems. They'd run some good races, but they hadn't gotten to where Junior thought they should be. He was paying more and more attention to them. It was sort of like a family where you have one kid who is struggling at school, and the parents start focusing on him so the other kid feels like he's being neglected. I'm not saying we were acting all childish about it. We were big boys and professionals. But in that operation, Junior was still the leader, and his attention was on the 12 car. We were drifting a little.

Then at Nashville in May, we had an ugly situation between the two teams that made the problem worse. We'd run a strong race and so had Bonnett and Geoffrey Bodine. Darrell caught Bodine with about 6 laps left in the race and was running in the lead when Kyle Petty and some others got into it. The caution came out on the white flag lap. Now the rule is pretty clear on this—you can't pass on the yellow so if you are the first car to the line for the last lap, and it is run under caution, then you win the race. It had been that way as long as anyone who was racing that day could remember.

But Bonnett passed Darrell on the last lap, and for some reason, NASCAR said it was a good pass and gave him the race. Junior went ballistic, Darrell went ape, and we were all screaming at the NASCAR people to read their own rule book. Meanwhile, the Bonnett team went to Victory Lane, and they were celebrating and carrying on. It was their first win. And right then, even though they were teammates, we felt like they were the enemy. It really caused some bad blood.

The next day, NASCAR ruled we'd won the race, but that didn't make things better between the two teams. Not entirely, anyway. That Nashville race was one more little thing in a season that was about a lot of little things.

Still, in early June after Pocono, we were tied with Terry Labonte for the points lead.

It would have helped us to win at Daytona on July 4th, but I think fate had other plans that day. We had a good car and all that, but there were bigger things than the points race at stake. We had the President of the United States coming down to Daytona to watch us race and to say the magic words, "Gentlemen, start your engines."

Ronald Reagan didn't make it to the race in time—the weather was a problem—so he patched in from Air Force One and gave the command over the radio, which was pretty cool. The fans, the drivers, and the crews were all pretty stoked. The race was on by the time President Reagan got to the grandstand, and it was looking like Richard Petty had a really fast car. To a lot of us down in the pits, the car looked like it might be a little on the small side, too. We thought that car might have been rebuilt and rejiggered to make it go fast enough for the King to win his 200th race, here at Daytona, in front of the President of the United States.

We were wondering what if he did win and during the teardown it came out that the car wasn't quite legal? What was NASCAR going to do? Take the race away from the King, after he'd won his 200th with the President watching?

Be interesting to find out.

We were out of it pretty early—even though we did manage to finish the race. Maybe because I didn't have a dog in the fight, I've got to say that it was one of the most exciting finishes I've ever seen at Daytona or anywhere else. The race came down to Cale Yarborough and Richard Petty—pretty good right there. They were together on the last lap under green, with Petty running just ahead and trying to hold Cale off. Cale tried to pull the slingshot, Petty dropped down on him, and they came down the straight banging and beating like the two old warriors that they were. Petty won it by a foot.

I'm told the President was really impressed. Petty drove to Victory Lane and then to the garage and the car never was inspected. Nobody was about to overrule *that* finish. It was an American classic.

After the race, President Reagan had a boxed chicken lunch with all of the drivers and the crews so I got to shake his hand. I was always a big admirer of his, and I think most of the other guys were, too. Even the old guys who'd been around and thought they couldn't be impressed were excited to meet him. I know I was.

Of course, with NASCAR just exploding and becoming so popular, it was inevitable that you'd have politicians, right up to the President, coming to races to cash in. The thing is, NASCAR people weren't always that happy to have them dropping by. A few years after that Daytona race, Bill Clinton came to Darlington to do a little politicking when he was running for president the first time. When he came through the garage area, most of the drivers and crew people were someplace else. Mark Martin got to be Clinton's escort that day, I guess because he was from Arkansas.

When he went out to be introduced to the fans, Clinton got booed pretty strong. I believe they thought he was a phony and that the people who were behind him weren't really friends of NASCAR and its values.

Just a guess, though. Could be they were just feeling a little rowdy. That happens at Darlington.

The week after that race at Daytona, we went to Nashville, which Darrell liked to call his "home track." He'd won 8 out of his last 18 races there, and we were pretty confident. Darrell ran a strong race but lost a close one to Geoffrey Bodine. The thing that was interesting about this was that it was the second time Bodine had won that season, and he was driving for a rookie owner.

Rick Hendrick was a really successful businessman from Charlotte who had built a Chevrolet dealership there into an empire. He decided he wanted to get into racing, and a lot of the guys who'd been around were kind of skeptical. We'd all seen it before with people like J.D. Stacey and M.C. Anderson, and we knew what the pattern was. They came in all full of themselves, thinking that because they had succeeded at something else they were going to start winning, right away, in racing. Then they learned that racing is hard, especially when you are up against people like Junior Johnson, Bud Moore, and the Wood brothers, who have made racing and winning their lives. It isn't some hobby or pastime with them.

Most of the time, these guys get discouraged and quit. Or they cut way back until they aren't really trying to win championships. They just want to be good enough to win the occasional race, or challenge, so they can keep living the racing life.

What I'm saying is, racing isn't in their blood.

So nobody was sure about Rick Hendrick. Could be he was another one of those guys, or maybe he was the real deal.

Well, that Nashville race was the second one Bodine had won that season, driving for Hendrick, so it was starting to look like he just might be the real deal. People in NASCAR were definitely taking notice. That included Darrell, who always kept his eyes and ears open.

Darrell and Rick Hendrick would get together in the future, and looking back on it now, it seems inevitable. After Nashville, though, I wasn't thinking that far ahead to predict the future. We were down 42 points in the Cup race to Dale Earnhardt, and I was worrying about the car and staying in the hunt.

Our streak at Bristol ended when Darrell got caught up in one of those wild wrecks they have there. Then we blew an engine at Darlington. So on the tracks where we'd won twice in the spring, we finished 21st and 40th. When we couldn't make it past 30 laps at Darlington, that might have been the low point.

We still weren't quite *there* as a team, and that's about as precise as I can get. Fans of racing know the cars and drivers really well. They might know something about a great crew chief like Waddell Wilson or Harry Hyde. They may have some idea of who the team owner is, especially if it is a Junior Johnson or the Wood brothers. But the hard thing for anyone on the outside to understand very deeply is just how much this is a team sport. Don't get me wrong—you can't win without a good driver or a good car. But having a good driver—or a good car—isn't always enough.

Dale Earnhardt's story is an example of that. Earnhardt struggled after he won his first points championship in 1980 and didn't win his second until 1986. Now Dale Earnhardt was the same driver during those years when he wasn't winning championships. He just wasn't in the right situation. Everyone learned for sure how good he *really* was when he wound up winning his seventh championship. By then, he was with Richard Childress, and he had the right team around him to make it happen.

What makes the "right team," is something that is hard to put your finger on. You hear people, when they talk about sports, discussing "team chemistry." No question that there is something to it. It is that old thing about the whole being more than the sum of its parts. The people you put together have to be able to work together. It isn't enough that everyone is good separately. You don't necessarily make a winner just by putting together a group of individual stars. Darrell learned this, a few years down the road, when he finally did hook up with Rick Hendrick.

On a good team, everyone is so focused on the common goal that you don't really have any individuals. And a good team takes on, in some subtle way, the identity of the leader. Understanding how to forge a team and being able to do it counts just as much in NASCAR as it does in other sports—maybe more. I think it speaks volumes about how important the team concept is in NASCAR that Joe Gibbs could leave the National Football League where he'd coached three Super Bowl Redskin teams, come into racing, and in a few years, have a Cup-winning team. Gibbs was new to racing and had a lot to learn about cars. But he knew about building teams and may have been the best in the world at it.

Junior Johnson knew cars as well as anyone, but he also knew how to build a team and make it work together and get wins. But he was struggling that season, trying to run two teams and make a tough ownership situation work. He eventually had to take Warner Hodgdon to court over money, and that, surely, had to be a distraction. Even Junior Johnson could lose focus and the little bit of focus that was missing from the operation that season cost us.

Not being able to finish 30 laps at Darlington pretty much said it all.

But good teams don't quit, even when they are struggling.

Driving back that night from Darlington, I felt about as low as I had in a long time. Everyone knows that in racing, you win 'em and you lose 'em. But you want to be in contention, and you want to be finishing races. You feel almost ashamed when you can't go out and race with the cars that are up front and contend and finish the race. I told myself, in the truck that night, that things were going to change. We might be just about out of it in the points, but we were not quitting, and we weren't getting embarrassed again.

Sometimes, when you feel like your back is against the wall, that's when you do your best work. I felt like we'd let Junior, Darrell, and ourselves down. We'd won four races—more than anyone else—but we were getting DNFs and finishing way down in the races we weren't winning, and that isn't the way a Junior Johnson race team did it.

We were back working on the car that next morning, and I made darn sure it was going to finish the race at Richmond and maybe do a little better than that.

And Darrell nosed out Ricky Rudd to win. We celebrated but not for very long. We still had something to prove. And 2 weeks later, we won again at Martinsville. We were still trailing pretty badly in the points. Darrell made some kind of statement about how he thought they should tinker with the points system. He'd won more races, and more money, than anyone, and it seemed like that ought to count for more than it did.

But the system was what it was. NASCAR could tinker with it— and it has over the years—but there are always going to be people who think it isn't fair. But it still comes down to how you do on the track. We were more than 200 points down, and the reality was we were pretty much out of it. But you can't let yourself think that way. You race to win, and, who knew, maybe we could win 'em all. That's the way I was thinking, right up until lap 182 at Charlotte the next week. That's when Darrell, who was running first, ran into a car that had spun out in front of him. After we got the car running again, we finished 27th.

There was no quit in our team, though. Darrell won his seventh race of the season the next week at North Wilkesboro.

Still Terry Labonte won the Cup that year. He won two races. But he was consistent, and we weren't. We finished fifth in the points and came back home from Riverside feeling like we definitely had something to prove.

*E*very now and then in sports, someone jumps over everyone else and leaves them eating his dust and playing catch-up. In early 1985, that's what it looked like had happened in NASCAR Winston Cup racing. Ford came out with a Thunderbird that was smaller than the GM cars. The shape of that car made it aerodynamically superior to everything else on the track—by a lot. The car was fast and

very hard to race against. Because of the shape, it was almost impossible to tuck in behind one of those Fords with a bigger car and draft. It just didn't leave a big enough hole in the air. You'd get back where you should have been carried along in the draft, and the air would be all dirty and rough. You'd get buffeted around like you were a ship in a storm.

And then, there was one team running Fords that managed to get even more out of them than anyone else. The team owner was

Harry Melling, and his crew chief and engine builder was Ernie Elliott, the brother of their driver. Bill Elliott was a sort of quiet, almost shy-looking guy but a real competitor in a race car. He was from a town in Georgia called Dawsonville, and it wasn't long before people started calling him "Awesome Bill from Dawsonville."

That season, everything just sort of came together for the Elliott brothers and the Melling team. They were—really and truly—awesome.

But sometimes slow and steady isn't a bad way to go. It turned out to be a hare and tortoise season. Because we were running Chevrolets, we got to be the tortoise.

Before the season started, we'd all been hearing about how fast those Fords were, but we got a real education at Daytona when Elliott laid down a qualifying lap that was more than 205 mph. Nobody had come close to that before. We figured our Chevrolets would just lose stability—almost like they were trying to take off and fly—at about 203 mph.

On race day, Elliott ran away from everybody. After one long pit stop, he had dropped behind the leader by about the length of one straightaway. He put his foot on the floor and had the lead again in less than 11 laps. Just ate the track up. Watching from the pits, we felt kind of helpless.

NASCAR made some rules changes about the dimensions of the car. The Chevys were now a little lower and the Fords a little higher. It was supposed to equalize things and make the competition more fair. Everybody was just hoping that those rule changes would slow down Awesome Bill. He had won three of the first eight races, in spite of breaking his leg in a wreck in the third race of the season.

That happened when he blew a tire at Rockingham and hit the wall. He had 2 weeks to get better before the next race. But Bill was still in pretty bad shape, so he had a relief driver standing by to take over after he started the race. But being in that fast car must have made him feel better because he stuck it out for 328 laps and won the Coca-Cola 500 at Atlanta.

The first race under the new rules was at Talladega, which is a plenty fast track, maybe the fastest on the NASCAR circuit. Everybody found out how much the new rules had slowed Elliott down when he went out and won the pole with a qualifying speed of 209 plus.

With Elliott's car running that fast, the best hope for the rest of us was for him to crash or break down. On the 48th lap, it looked like we got our wish. Elliott went into the pits trailing smoke. By the time he got the problem fixed—some kind of oil seal, I believe—they were down almost 2 laps, and the race was still under green.

So Elliott came back out on the track, down in the race by about 5 miles, and he started picking 'em off. He went by car after car like he just wouldn't be denied. Every lap was 204 or 205. Up ahead, the lead kept changing, and Elliott just kept coming until, finally, he had made up the whole 5 miles and was back in the lead. It was one of the greatest comebacks anyone had ever seen in NASCAR racing.

Now if you were trying to compete with Elliott, you obviously had a problem. A lot of guys tried to keep up with him, and they just couldn't do it. They also wore out their own cars trying. That's what happened to us at Talladega. We actually led 1 whole lap, but we burned up a piston and got a DNF.

The other strategy for beating Elliott was to run your own race, try to keep your car in one piece, and maybe get lucky at the end. You could hope that he'd run into trouble of some kind and give you a chance to sneak in the back door. But we'd all seen just how well that worked at Talladega.

Still, that seemed like the smart play. We decided to keep trying to make our car run a little faster and, at the same time, make sure it could stay in the race and finish. We operated on the old Junior Johnson philosophy that had never been improved on. And still hasn't. You run to win, and if you can't win, you go for a top five or ten. And if you can't do that, then you hang in there and finish the race.

So, for the rest of the season, we were doing what golfers call "grinding it out." If it had been football, we would have been trying to win with defense and the kicking game.

After Talladega, we went to Dover. Bill Elliott won the race—lapped the field, ho-hum—but we managed a fourth place finish. We were running sixth in the points, 134 behind Elliott. It felt like it was further than that.

So we went to Charlotte for an unusual weekend. The 600-mile Memorial Day race is always one of the biggest on the NASCAR calendar, and that year it was even bigger than usual. Bill Elliott, who had to be the favorite going into the race, stood to make some real money if he did win. One million dollars to be exact.

This was a promotional prize that R.J. Reynolds had put up for any driver who won three of what everybody considered the big four Winston Cup races: the Daytona 500, the Talladega Winston 500, the 600 at Charlotte, and the Southern 500 on Labor Day at Darlington. Elliott had already won the first two legs, and it didn't look like anyone could beat him. Especially not on a superspeedway. At the garage, there were already guys asking him if they could borrow some of that million.

There was also going to be a non-Cup race at Charlotte that Memorial Day weekend. It would be an all-star race called "the Winston." Drivers who'd won the year before would race for 105 laps, and the winner would take home $200,000. Elliott was in the race so he had a chance to make $1.2 million that weekend, plus whatever he took in prize and lap money from the 600.

We couldn't win the million, obviously, but we had a shot at the $200,000, and maybe that was the incentive we needed. Or maybe we were just frustrated with not having won a race yet and here it was almost June. Whatever it was, we went to Charlotte ready to race.

Elliott was, surprisingly, not a factor in the Winston. Maybe his mind was on other things—like the million. Darrell Waltrip ran hard and led early, but late in the race he got behind. With 10 laps to go, he was still trailing Harry Gant by 3 seconds. Junior got on the radio and said something about the $200,000. That must have gotten Darrell's attention. He finally got ahead of Gant in turn four of the last lap. Beat him by about three-tenths of a second.

The engine blew just as he was crossing the finish line.

Things kept on going our way the next day. The pressure of winning that million was on Elliott, who had won the pole, but he didn't have a very good day. He was in and out of the pits with a car that just wasn't right. He finished 18th. Meanwhile, Darrell had to catch Gant—again—late in the race, and he did it.

So we went to Victory Lane twice in 2 days. Darrell got booed both times, but there was something in the way the fans did it that made you think they'd missed him.

Jaws was back.

We'd won two races in 2 days, but only got Cup points for one. Elliott shook off the Charlotte slump and won two straight weekends on superspeedways—Pocono and Michigan. We did what we could, stayed close. Took a third at Pocono and a second at Michigan. That kept us 86 points behind Elliott, so we were still in the hunt.

We were right behind him again at Daytona on the Fourth of July, and a journeyman driver named Greg Sacks was ahead of both of us in one of the biggest upsets in NASCAR history.

It turned out later on that Sacks had been running a big engine. But no matter, the race was history by then and in the books.

Elliott won at Pocono; Darrell ran third. We were starting to see a pattern here. We couldn't beat him, but we could stay close, and in a long season who knew what might happen. Nobody on our team was quitting or even getting discouraged. We knew what the challenge was, and we felt like we were up to it. We were going to keep the pressure on Elliott to keep winning and just see if he could hold up under it.

When Elliott won again at Michigan in August, Darrell was right behind him. Didn't even lose any ground in the points race.

Darrell, as usual, had something to say about the situation. And even if you didn't like him, you had to admire him for being consistent.

"We feel fortunate," he said, "to be this close—just 143 points behind. Bill should be much further ahead. I've said all along that the system needs some adjustment. You don't get enough points for winning a race."

Still we didn't make the rules. We just had to go out and play by them.

The stretch run started at Darlington on Labor Day. The Southern 500 is always a great race, one that has always drawn the real, hard corps of NASCAR fans. Something about that track and that race and that holiday just speaks to them. There is as much electricity in the air at that race as there is at Daytona.

And this year there was an extra measure of excitement because the Winston Million was on the line. This would be Elliott's last chance to win it, and the pressure was on. The press was all over the story, and Bill and his team had a hard time being left alone in the garage. NASCAR eventually had to put uniformed policemen down there to keep people out so Elliott and his team could do their work. When you did see those guys, you could tell it was getting to them. They had the look.

But, then, a million dollars plus Darlington would be enough to make anyone tighten up.

They seemed to have a good car when the race started. And they led the first few laps. But then Elliott fell back, and he was coming close to going a lap down when a caution came out. Elliott got some setup help in the pits, and he was running better when he got back on the track.

But he still had to race Cale Yarborough. That's no day at the beach anywhere and particularly not at Darlington. Elliott did his best racing on superspeedways, like Daytona and Talladega. But he also had a really fine touch, and that was a big asset at Darlington where you had to feel your way around the track and stay on the edge but also stay out of trouble. Elliott drove a smooth, smart race, and he hung on Cale's bumper.

When Yarborough had power steering problems and went in to the pits, Elliott got into the lead and after that, he just held on. Cale was racing for the win and that was all it took to get him charging. He stood to make about fifty grand if he won the race; Elliott was looking at the million. Elliottt ran a good, smart, tough race against the best competition around and took the checkered flag by a little over half a second. The million was his, he'd earned it, and the pressure was off.

Or was it?

After Darlington, Elliott was leading in the Cup race by 206 points, with eight races left. Nobody on our team was feeling like we had 'em right where we wanted 'em. But then, Elliott's team seemed like it was drained. They'd won 10 races and the Winston Million, and it didn't seem like they had anything left for the points race.

So far, we'd won just one race. We were still hungry. We wanted that championship.

"It's a long road," Darrell said, "but we've been here before."

We felt like predators, stalking Elliott.

We caught him the very next weekend at Richmond. Won the race while he finished 12th. That cut his lead in the points by about 25 percent, right there.

We went to Dover and ran second to Harry Gant. But Elliott had another tough race and finished 20th. Now we were 86 points behind and closing fast.

We came in a close second to Dale Earnhardt at Martinsville. Elliott finished 17th. The lead was now 23 points.

When Elliott dropped a transmission in the next race, we caught him, even though we had our own problems—bad distributor—and couldn't really close the deal. When the race was over, we were leading the Cup race by 33 points.

Elliott got some of that back the next week at Charlotte. He ran second to Cale Yarborough, and we came in fourth. Our lead was now just 20 points.

This thing was getting *good*.

The next week, we won the race at Rockingham when Darrell hid in the weeds and stayed out of trouble until the last 100 miles of the race. It wasn't the kind of track where Elliott could let that racehorse of his just run. He finished fourth. We were up 35 in the points race.

Thinking back on it, I believe that's when I knew we had him. You just get a feeling, when you are a competitor, for when your opponent has lost it. He might still be standing and going through the motions, but you've won the race or the fight or the game. You know it, he knows it, and you know he knows it.

We'd won on our kind of track, at Rockingham. Now we just had to stay close on Elliott's kind of track in Atlanta. Then we'd go out to California and finish it on a road course at Riverside. I felt confident, and so did everybody on the team. We were up, the same way we'd been back when Cale was running Darrell down, a few seasons back.

We still felt confident after Elliott won at Atlanta. It was a really remarkable achievement. It was the 11th race he'd won that year (we'd won three). He'd won them all on superspeedways, and that broke a record. David Pearson had won 10 big track races in 1973. No question about it, this had been a great year for Elliott.

But, by the way, we finished third, behind Cale Yarborough, and were still up by 20 in the points after the Atlanta race. There was a lot more discussion in the papers and on the radio about how unfair the whole thing was and how tough it was on Elliott. And a part of me does agree that there is something about a points system that has a driver who wins three races ahead of a driver who wins 11 that seems *unfair*, I suppose.

We didn't make any new friends—and probably added some enemies to what was already a pretty big crowd—by winning the points. Everybody wanted Elliott to have the complete, super season, and we were raining on his parade. And it is easy to understand those feelings.

But what nobody was saying at the time was that Bill Elliott had a car that was just flying around those tracks while the rest of us were struggling, trying to find a way to keep up with him and win anything we could. We were the underdogs. Darrell was sort of the *Rocky* character in this particular script, and it would have been easy *not* to hang in there and run hard for second or third place while Elliott was laying down lap records and winning the big races from here to as far as you could see. Bill had a great season; no denying that. But we were the wildcard team that hung in there and made it through the playoffs and then beat the favorite in the Super Bowl. We weren't the glamour team. We did it on desire and hard work.

Winning is never easy, no matter how you do it. But winning when you are coming from behind and the other guy has the faster car, that says something about your team's character.

We went out to California, confident that we'd win it however we had to. And it turned out to be easier than we'd expected. Elliott had transmission problems early on, and he never really contended. He finished 31st in a race where he had to do well. Darrell stroked it and came in seventh. We won the Cup by 101 points, which was really a kind of rout. It was the biggest lead in more than 10 years. That still didn't sit right with some people, but I thought Darrell Waltrip, of all people, put the right sort of gracious note on it.

"The way it turned out," Darrell said, "it means two guys have had successful seasons."

Going into the 1986 season, we felt pretty confident that we weren't going to be blindsided the way we'd been by the Fords in '85. The rules had been changed around by NASCAR, and we had arrived at what other sports like to call "parity" again as far as the equipment was concerned.

So we had reason to feel pretty good about things. If the cars

were going to be equal, well, then we knew we had the driver and the team to be competitive, at least. We'd proved that we could win the points when we were at a disadvantage. With things evened out, we should be able to do it again and win a few more races along the way.

But you never know what new obstacles are on the horizon, or what old obstacles that you'd thought you were done with might still be lurking around and coming back to bite you on the butt. Turned out that while we had the car and the team, we had a driver whose mind was on bigger things. NASCAR was going through something like what baseball experienced with free agency. The old loyalties didn't exist anymore, and it was almost to the point of every man for himself. The money was there, and people felt like they didn't have any choice but to go for it.

There was also some new competition from one of the most charismatic drivers NASCAR had seen in a long time. We all learned about him that year and thought we were going to be hearing from him for years and years to come. Didn't happen that way, though. What started as one of the most exciting *A Star is Born* sort of stories turned into *Bang the Drum Slowly*.

But let's go back and start where we always do. At Daytona.

Once more, we didn't win the Daytona 500. But we didn't have anything to be ashamed of, coming in third. That was getting to be a habit we wanted to break. It was our third consecutive third place finish.

The driver who had the real good news/bad news story of the week was the one we figured would be our strongest competition that year—Dale Earnhardt. In fact, I believe if you'd polled all the NASCAR fans at the start of that season about who they thought were the strongest drivers in Cup racing, it would have been a dead heat between Darrell Waltrip and Dale. At that time, they were the two superstars of the sport.

Earnhardt looked like he was going to blow through Daytona like a hurricane. He won the Busch Clash. Then he won his 125-mile qualifying race. Then he won the 300-mile Sportsman race. He was just dominating Speedweeks.

Earnhardt looked dominant on race day, too. He'd survived a lot of wrecks in the early part of the race and was drafting Geoff Bodine, who was in the lead with 3 laps to go. You could almost see Earnhardt sizing Bodine up, taking his measure, and figuring just exactly where he was going to make his move on the last lap to get around him. Then Earnhardt ran out of gas.

Earnhardt had to pit, of course, and it dropped him so far back he finished the race at 14th. But that was Dale. He raced to win.

We learned that the next week, at Richmond, and learned it good and hard.

We were running the old Fairgrounds track back then. It was a flat, half-miler where you raced old-style, and there was always a lot of banging and beating. The smart drivers would lie back and pick their spots, and that's what it looked like Darrell was going to do.

Junior Johnson was watching the race from on top of a truck that was parked down near the pits. He could see the whole track from up there, and he was watching everything. It was getting down to the last 10 laps or so, and Darrell was chasing Earnhardt, looking to pass him. Earnhardt kept moving around, blocking him. It was pretty clear that Darrell had the faster car, but getting around Earnhardt was going to be the trick. I couldn't see everything that was going on from down in the pit. I just heard Junior whenever he'd get on the radio. But, as usual, he wasn't doing much talking.

Then with about 3 laps to go, I heard Junior say over the radio, "Okay, boy. Pass him, *now*."

And Darrell did it. He made a really neat move and got around Earnhardt, like he'd been setting him up for it, and then he had the lead coming out of the backstretch. It didn't look like there was any way Earnhardt could catch him.

And there wasn't. But that didn't mean Dale couldn't *wreck* him.

That's exactly what he did. Earnhardt was trying to pass high, and he couldn't—no way. So Earnhardt put his nose into the right rear quarter panel of Darrell's car and spun him right up into the wall. Hard. Just demolished the car and knocked the wind out of Darrell.

"The son of a bitch wrecked him," Junior said into the radio.

He was quiet for a couple of seconds. I guess he was looking to see if Darrell was okay because nothing was coming through the radio. It must have been knocked loose in the wreck.

After a while Junior said, "Jeff, get your crew and go on down there. Look after your driver."

I think he meant that if Darrell needed help, we were supposed to help him, and if Darrell wanted to fight, we were supposed to back him up and take on anyone who tried to get into it on the other side.

We went down there all right. But even though Darrell had gotten the car back out on the track and tried to run down Earnhardt and smack him, Darrell wasn't in any shape to fight.

That didn't mean he wasn't mad. Darrell made his feelings plain, and so did Junior and so did a lot of other people who weren't really involved.

NASCAR looked at the films and came down pretty hard. They fined Earnhardt $5,000, put him on probation for a year, and made him put up a $10,000 bond if he wanted to keep racing. It was about as drastic as anything anyone could remember.

Earnhardt fought it. He kept saying that it was just a racing accident and the whole thing was a case of "driver error." When he said, flat out, that he hadn't tried to wreck Darrell, I lost a lot of respect for him. He'd been my friend, but things cooled off a lot between us after that. What bothered me even more than what he'd done was that he was denying what everybody watching could see was the truth. He wanted this reputation as "the Intimidator," and he was doing everything he could to get it. But he was being coy about it, and it rubbed me wrong.

NASCAR heard Earnhardt's appeal and eventually dropped the probation and the deal about posting bond. They usually do. Those fines get a lot of publicity. Nobody says anything when they are dropped on appeal.

I think part of the reason is that aggressive driving is what fans want, so NASCAR has to walk a really fine line. On one hand, they've got to discourage the dangerous stuff, and they don't want the sport to turn into a demolition derby. On the other hand, they don't want to eliminate aggressive driving and lose the fans.

There was no question that Earnhardt drove aggressively—to put it mildly—all of his career. I'll say this for him, he wasn't out there trying to settle scores and just be a bad ass for the sake of it. There was a strategy to what he was doing. Most of the time, when he hit you it was because he wanted to get you out of the way so he could win a race. And after a while, when he'd gotten the reputation for doing it, there were times when he didn't have to hit someone. They'd see him coming and get out of the way.

Earnhart made that reputation work for him. He got a lot of people mad, and a lot of people tried to get even with him. And there were times when he crossed the line from hard racing to dangerous racing. One of them was that wreck at Richmond; no question about it. If somebody ever does a collection of "Dale Earnhardt's Greatest Hits," that one is going to be included, I guarantee you.

People today will talk to me about Earnhardt's way of driving like it is something that has gone out of style. But the truth is, you see a lot of guys out there today who know how to do what he did without drawing a lot of attention to themselves. There are also some, like Tony Stewart, who don't mind letting people know they'll knock you out of the way if they can't get around you.

It would surprise a lot of people to know that Jeff Gordon is one of the best out there at doing what I call "the bump and run." I've seen him do it to Rusty Wallace two or three times. But because Gordon is everybody's idea of Mr. Clean, nobody makes a big deal out of it.

But believe me, Jeff Gordon will put it to you if you are between him and winning the race.

Another thing about racing today compared to the time when Earnhardt was making his reputation is that you can do some things without ever even making contact. There are drivers out there—Jeff Gordon, again—who are skillful enough to use the air to get another car loose. They ease up close on a guy's left rear and break up the flow of air coming around the car just enough to reduce the downforce and get the tires loose for that split second. You see it again and again. You can spin the guy without even touching him.

In the end, NASCAR has always been about racing hard, and if you take that element out of it, you've lost something that is vital to the sport. We've got some tracks now where the speeds are so fast that it is always dangerous when cars touch. And at places like Talladega, they put restrictor plates on the carburetors to reduce the air flow, cut horsepower, and slow everybody down. It is done for safety, but what has happened is that all the cars are now running at the same speed, and nobody can pass. So you have this big, tight herd of cars going around the track at 200 mph. When a couple of them do touch, you get a huge wreck that takes out 10 or more cars. At Talladega, you go into the race worrying about "the big one."

You expect wrecks at Bristol, too. But they aren't as catastrophic when they happen, and a good team can make the tight racing and the possibility of chaos work for it. The short tracks are where the pure, old dirt-track style of racing lives on, and I hope we have some of that forever.

Once all the emotions and the dust had settled after the Richmond race, everybody got back to racing. We were actually leading in the points late in April, but we weren't winning any races. It was pretty clear that Earnhardt had the horses. He ran away from everybody at Darlington.

And while Earnhardt and his team had the momentum, we were struggling. The problem, in this case, wasn't with the car, with Junior being distracted, or with any of those things. It was, pure and simple, the driver. Darrell had started looking around and talking to people. He didn't want to be driving for Junior Johnson anymore.

It was sort of a replay of what he'd been through with DiGard—but not exactly. Back then, Darrell had one of the best contracts in racing, but he didn't quite have the ride to win championships. He was still young, and he was hungry. He wanted to hear people say he was the best almost as much as he wanted the money.

Well, Darrell came over to Junior, and he won three championships in 5 years. There was no telling how many more championships he might win now because he had the ride. Junior Johnson ran a winning operation.

So this time with Darrell it wasn't the ride; it was the money.

Junior felt that if he had a deal with you, then that was the deal. You might think you were worth more—and you could be right—but you still had a deal. There was a lot of new money coming into NASCAR. And the people with the money who were coming in were willing to spend it, right now, to put together a winning team. Darrell saw other drivers getting rich, and they hadn't done anything close to what he'd done.

Junior's thinking was, *That might be true, but we've still got a contract.*

Now anybody who was out to build a winner quick, no question about the cost, would have just loved to get his hands on Darrell Waltrip. You'd have the cornerstone of a winning operation in place, right there. And if you were shopping around for other parts of the package—say a very lucrative, high-profile sponsorship—then you'd be using the name of a superstar driver as a way to make the sale.

These discussions might have started off as private negotiations, but they didn't stay secret very long. There was no way they could. Darrell's name was being shopped.

And we knew early in the season that Darrell was testing the market. Junior's attitude about these things was always the same. He felt that if you didn't want to be around, then he didn't want you around. I imagine he was hoping that Darrell would go on and leave in the middle of the season, so he could get on with finding a new driver.

But Darrell didn't leave. He stayed, and things got brittle and cold around the shop. We still talked, but it was like we were business associates, not teammates. Instead of getting together to figure things out about the car, Junior and Darrell tried to avoid each other when they could. If they had to talk, it was cool and formal.

So we went from being a great, close unit that could rise to a challenge to a good, functioning group missing that last little ingredient that puts you over the top. We were all good enough at what we did that we might have been able to win, even without that spirit and that closeness, but we were up against two teams that had what we were missing.

One of those was the Richard Childress operation with Dale Earnhardt driving and Kirk Shelmerdine as his crew chief. They had that intangible thing—chemistry—that gets you winning and makes it habit. And, of course, they became one of the great teams in NASCAR history.

The other one was a new team, and a really unlikely one at that.

Rick Hendrick—the Charlotte automobile dealer who'd gotten into racing and done well with Geoff Bodine—was the owner. The crew chief was Harry Hyde, who was a real old pro. The driver was a young guy from Ohio with a great smile and an appetite for the good life and the parties like no one in NASCAR since, maybe, Curtis Turner.

Tim Richmond could drive, and he could party. He didn't hold anything back when he was doing either one of those things. It was always full out. And he had one of the great, winning personalities of all time. If you were around him, you liked him. He seemed to like everybody, and there was just no question that he enjoyed life. But he was a really different sort of cat around the NASCAR scene—definitely not your blue jean–wearing, pickup truck–driving redneck. Tim liked Armani suits, and sometimes he'd come to the track in a limo. He went out with movie stars, women who wanted to be movie stars, and some women who just looked like movie stars. Tim liked the ladies.

The Hendrick/Hyde/Richmond team didn't look like it was going to work, at first. In the first 10 races of the '86 season, Tim had one top five and finished 20th or lower four times. He was not lighting up the tracks.

Then at the 600 over Memorial Day, Tim finished second, behind Earnhardt. After that, he took off like a comet. In the last 19 races of the season, Tim won seven times and came in second four times. He finished out of the top 10 in only four races. I believe it was the most phenomenal streak of racing in NASCAR history. It certainly beat anything I'd ever seen.

This wasn't like the year before, when Bill Elliott was winning with equipment that was clearly superior and doing it all in one kind of environment—namely, superspeedways. Richmond was doing this with great driving, and he was winning on everything—superspeedways, short tracks, and road courses. We thought we had the best road course driver, and we were sure we knew how to build a car for a road course. But when we went to Watkins Glen in August, Richmond ran Darrell down with about 10 laps to go and won the race. He'd won the Firecracker 400 at Daytona. He drove a great race at Darlington and beat Bobby Allison by 2 seconds. People had said Tim wasn't really good on the short tracks, but he beat Earnhardt at Richmond, on the same track where Dale had punted us.

If you hadn't been racing against him, then it would have been thrilling to watch Tim Richmond race that season.

Unfortunately, we *were* racing against him, and we were having our troubles. We were managing to hang on to a lead in the points, right up until the end of April, even though we hadn't won any races. Then Earnhardt got ahead of us with a third at Talladega when we got a DNF.

We finally got our first win at Riverside on the 1st of June, but by then Darrell's discontent was infecting the team. We won again at Bristol in late August, after an Earnhardt crash opened the door. Earnhardt tried to bump a lapped car to get him out of the way and managed to spin himself into the wall. We liked that almost as much as we liked winning the race. The win moved us back up to second in the points to where we had a theoretical chance of catching Earnhardt. We were 121 points down, and we'd come from further back than that to catch Elliott.

We might have looked like a slick, professional NASCAR operation and the defending Winston Cup champions, but that was just appearances. Behind the scenes, things weren't going the way they do in a winning, confident operation. At one point, my knee started giving me trouble. In a different situation, I would have waited until the off-season to get it operated on. But Junior told me to go ahead and have the surgery. So I worked several races in a cast, and we got somebody to fill in for me on the jack. You don't do that if you're all on the same page and trying to win together.

It got so bad that when Junior and I were discussing how to set the car up for the September race at Dover, I said something about how I thought doing it a certain way might work, except that Darrell wouldn't go for it.

"Do it anyway and don't tell him," Junior said. "We need to find out what's going to work best for the next driver we put in the car."

So I set the car up the way Junior wanted me to and didn't tell Darrell. We didn't do that well in the race—finished 14th, I believe— but it wasn't because of the setup. The transmission was squirrelly and gave us problems all day. Darrell never said anything about the chassis setup.

Darrell pulled out one more win in late September. He got it at North Wilkesboro, and I suppose you could say it was ironic because that's Junior Johnson country. By then it had been announced that Darrell was leaving Junior and going to drive for Rick Hendrick.

Darrell was gracious in the press. He thanked Junior and Flossie and said his time with them had been "the best 6 years of my life."

He'd won 53 races and three championships running in Junior Johnson's number 11 car. The car was still plenty good, and Junior hadn't lost anything. The team was, hands down, still one of the best in Winston Cup racing. Even with all the turmoil and bad feelings, we would wind up finishing Darrell's last season second in the points race behind Earnhardt (a long way) and just ahead of Tim Richmond, who had won more races than either of us.

So if the team was still one of the best and the owner and his family had treated Darrell so well, why go off and join up with another, un-proven operation?

The answer to that one is really simple. It was the money.

Rick Hendrick is a superb businessman and dealmaker, and during the '86 season he had been working hard to put together his new team. He needed a great driver, and he got that in Darrell. But he also needed a big-time sponsor, and he got that, too, when he went to Procter & Gamble and landed Tide. He needed them both to make the thing work.

Now most people wouldn't have thought of a laundry detergent as a likely sponsor for a NASCAR team. When you thought about racing and sponsors, you thought automotive products like STP, Petty's sponsor. Or beer, maybe. We had the Budweiser car that year. Then you thought of tobacco products like the number 55 Copenhagen smokeless tobacco car that Benny Parsons drove. Those were all kind of male-oriented products. There were a few sponsors that weren't what you'd call gender specific. Like Kodak and Hardee's and Folgers coffee, Tim Richmond's sponsor. Interestingly, Richmond also drove for Hendrick.

But Tide laundry detergent seemed like the sort of product that only women bought or thought about.

And, of course, that was the genius of the deal. There were a lot of women who went to NASCAR races or watched them on television. Plenty of them were serious fans, of course, but a lot of them were watching because their husbands or boyfriends did. But they *were* watching, and when they saw that the winning car had the Tide logo and paint scheme, it had to influence them. It was a way for Tide to reach a market.

But maybe more important, it was a way for NASCAR to broaden the brand. That was the whole strategy behind the way the sport grew in the '80s and '90s. The old image of a bunch of tough good-old-boys who learned to drive by hauling moonshine was far too narrow and negative if the sport was going to expand and grow beyond the original Southern base. It had to attract people from all over the country and all classes of people. And it couldn't just ignore half the population.

That's why Humpy Wheeler had pushed so hard for Janet Guthrie to drive in NASCAR. Getting a big, high-profile sponsorship from Tide was another way of accomplishing the same thing. It helped sell NASCAR to mainstream America.

It probably sold a lot of soap, too.

Certainly it made for one of the most spectacular car rollouts you've ever seen. Hendrick introduced what he called the "Tide Ride" at the Charlotte Motor Speedway in the off-season that year. They had a big light show, and the car came blasting through one of those big paper curtains. Painted in that trademark bright orange, that Chevrolet was a real show-stopper.

Hendrick had lined up Waddell Wilson as crew chief. Wilson was a legend, going back to his days with Holman Moody, when his driver was David Pearson and his crew was made up of people who were supposed to be the best at whatever it was they did. They called it "The Dream Team," and they got to that name before O.J. started hiring lawyers.

Hendrick promoted the whole deal to a fare-thee-well, and it was talked about all around NASCAR. Some reporter was talking to Darrell, who never could resist a chance to talk, and he started talking about how great it all was.

"I finally got me a thoroughbred," Darrell said.

Another reporter told Junior what Darrell had said.

"I don't know about any thoroughbred," Junior said. "I do know we had us a jackass around here who recently left."

Junior had business of his own to take care of. He had to hire a new driver, and he went with Terry Labonte. Terry was about as far in temperament from Darrell Waltrip as you could get. He was quiet, for one thing.

Labonte had an ego, like all drivers, but he had a way of keeping a lid on it. He was kind of laid back that way. He didn't assert himself a lot, and maybe because we'd all been around Darrell so long, and keyed off of him, that actually got to be a little bit of a problem. We were used to hearing from our driver about what he wanted and what he thought we needed to do to the car. Terry didn't give us a lot of input. We'd tell him about something we were thinking about doing to the car, and he'd say, "Sounds good to me."

With Darrell it would have been an hour of conversation and maybe an argument. That got to be the way we made decisions, through lots and lots of discussion and argument. With Terry, we weren't getting that feedback. Funny, we'd complained about it before, but then we missed it.

But Terry Labonte was a great driver. No question about it. He'd won the Cup in 1984. That was the year Darrell won seven races. Labonte only won two, but he was more consistent than we were. In fact, he may have been one of the most consistent, steady drivers in NASCAR history. He had a great career that included a streak of 655 consecutive starts, and he later went on to win another Cup in 1996 when he was driving for Rick Hendrick.

My feelings for Darrell Waltrip went all over the place, sometimes in 10 minutes or less. But I never felt anything but an enormous respect for Terry Labonte.

I just wish we could have had more success together.

The problems we ran into in '87 didn't have anything to do with the driver or the owner. They might have had something to do with the crew chief situation—namely the fact that we had two of them.

I was one, and the other was Tim Brewer. Junior set it up that way when he closed down the Neil Bonnett ride in the number 12 car and went back to racing just one car—the number 11 with Labonte driving. Tim Brewer had been crew chief on the Bonnett ride, and Junior didn't want to let either of us go. It was a complicated situation and Junior had his reasons. He always did, and I sure wasn't going to be the one to question Junior Johnson. His solution was to bring Tim over to the 11 car and set up a situation where we'd have two crew chiefs. One of us would do short tracks, and the other would do the superspeedways. I did the big tracks.

It was another one of Junior's innovations—like the way he had me staying in the shop and building cars to keep me away from Darrell in 1981.

That had turned out to be a slick way of solving a nagging problem. But nobody's perfect, and this time, Junior's solution didn't work so well.

Something else was going on during that off-season—something that didn't directly concern our team and that nobody in NASCAR knew anything about. Just the same, it was an event that would rock the sport.

Right after he'd won the last race of the season, at Riverside, Tim Richmond went back to Ohio and checked into the Cleveland Clinic under a false name. He was a sick man, and he knew it. He probably knew what was making him sick and didn't want to admit it—not to himself and not to the world.

When Tim announced that he wouldn't be driving the first races in the '87 season, he said it was because he'd had double pneumonia and had come close to dying from it. It was going to take some time for him to completely recover.

The truth was Tim Richmond had AIDS.

But it was a long time before anyone knew—or even suspected— the truth. Nobody thought that much about it at the time, not knowing what was really going on. We had racing on our minds.

I don't have a lot of good memories from the '87 season. I was now in my second decade of Cup racing. In all that time, I'd worked for one owner—Junior Johnson. Since I started working for him, we'd won six championships and come in second three times. I'd been crew chief for two of those championship seasons.

So I don't think I'm exaggerating when I say I'd been to the top of

the NASCAR mountain. And I know I'm not exaggerating when I say that I liked the view from up there.

But nothing remains the same in this life, and nobody stays on top forever. I was about to learn that. I thought I could stick around Junior's and make it work. But things got off to a bad start between me and Tim Brewer, and they never got much better.

Darrell Waltrip had been talking to me ever since he went over to Rick Hendrick about leaving Junior and going with him.

"We got something good going here," he'd say. "You ought to get in on it while it's still early."

"I don't want to work for Waddell Wilson," I said. "Nothing against Waddell, personally, but I'm used to being the boss."

Waddell had a reputation for not sharing responsibility. Truth is, most good crew chiefs don't. We're particular that way.

It's a funny job, crew chief, and there isn't really any textbook you can use to find out what exactly you are supposed to do. It's one of those jobs where there isn't any job description. What you do is whatever needs to be done.

When I was crew chief for the number 11 car at Junior's, I did everything, including helping him bury his coon dogs and plant his garden. A big part of my job was running the shop, and that meant ordering parts and keeping things we needed in stock. I worked on the cars—building them, getting them set up, and repairing them. I worked on the engine and the tires. I did bodywork, and sometimes I worked on the paint scheme. I was involved in *anything* having to do with the car. To me, some of the best times during the week were when I'd taken care of all the administrative things and could actually start working on the car.

The other stuff was always coming up, and there were a hundred different things that I was responsible for: getting uniforms for the crew, getting a laundry service to take care of the dirty uniforms, answering the phone, and handling the mail. I refereed personnel problems in the shop. I hired, and, when necessary, I fired. I kept Junior informed about what was going on, and I had to deal with—and sometimes babysit—the driver. I also did things to keep the sponsor happy, such as make sure the logos were on the uniforms and the cars.

It was also my job to make sure that we were all functioning as a team and working together. As a crew chief, you have to make sure you don't get lazy and lose focus, and you also have to keep everyone from getting wound too tight. It was very possible to work too hard. Now and then, people would need some relief, and it would be up to me to find some way to break the tension, the way Junior had when he took us down the river in inner tubes, drinking moonshine and telephoning catfish.

I had different ways of doing that. I'd organize softball games during lunch breaks. If it was somebody's birthday, I'll pay for a stripper from Charlotte to come to the shop to do a strip and sing *Happy Birthday*. Sometimes, when I could tell everyone was getting too tight, I'd order a stripper and just tell somebody, "Congratulations, it's your birthday today. This year, you get two of them."

The traveling arrangements were a big part of my responsibilities. I had to make sure we packed everything we needed when we got ready to leave for a race and that we got there on time and in one piece. I made sure of the hotel reservations, and I even assigned roommates. I checked to make sure everyone got his per diem.

Finally it would be race day, and that would be the payoff.

I liked to get to the track early in the morning when it was cool and so quiet you couldn't believe it, especially when you knew how loud it would get later. I'd spend those first couple of quiet hours going over things, double-checking my notes, and walking around looking the car over. Maybe I'd go out and walk around the pit area and even up and down the track a little just so I could get a feel for things.

Later in the day, there would be meetings with NASCAR people and with the driver and a lot of things to attend to. The closer we got to the race, the busier I would get. But some days, if I wasn't too busy, I'd go to the infield chapel for the church services.

It seemed like the closer we got to the starting time, the more things there were to do, the more people who needed to talk to me about something, and the more decisions I had to make. Then, when they finally dropped the flag and we were actually racing, that's when I got *really* busy. And that's also when I *really* started having fun.

I was in charge of calling the race—keeping track of our lap times, fuel, and tire wear; talking to my driver and my spotter; following the other teams to see how they were doing and when they were coming into the pits; deciding when we were going to pit and how many tires we'd take on each stop, and watching the weather and track conditions. I was constantly trying to think it all through and stay on top of everything.

It was exhausting and incredibly rewarding. But I always said that at the end of the race, I wanted to feel just as tired and wrung out as my driver. Otherwise, I didn't feel like I'd done my job. You just couldn't believe the adrenaline pump. Especially if we won.

These days, each team has more people, doing more specialized jobs. It isn't the collaboration it was when I was first a crew chief. A lot of teams divide up the responsibilities so the guy who is working on the car is not the same guy taking care of hotel reservations and uniforms. They have somebody to take care of the administrative stuff, a team manager or something.

But back then, the crew chief did it all, and I'd gotten used to doing it that way. So I didn't want to start taking orders from Waddell Wilson or anyone else.

I told Darrell I was going to stay put and see how things worked out for me at Junior's under the new arrangement.

But here's the long and short of it—things didn't work out. Tim Brewer and I probably wouldn't have gotten along unless we'd both won every race we were responsible for. And even then there would probably have been some backbiting. As it was, we didn't win every race. In fact, we didn't win any. So there were problems, finger-pointing, and a lot of whispering around the shop.

By the time we got to Talladega in early May, I was starting to feel pretty good about my side of things. We'd run fourth at Atlanta about a month earlier, the last big track we raced on before Talladega. Since then, I'd been building a car specifically for Talladega. We'd taken the car down there, and we'd tried some different things and done a lot of testing. By the time we were through, we thought we had a pretty hot package. We figured they'd hear from us that day.

NASCAR fans remember that Talladega race for the bad wreck where Bobby Allison got loose, went into the air, and came down on a fence that ran along the grandstand. Parts of the car went everywhere. The debris got into the crowd, and several of the spectators were hurt. It was so bad they red-flagged the race for more than 2 hours while they took care of the injured people, cleaned up the debris, and repaired the fence.

Davey Allison was driving in his rookie season, and he saw that wreck in his rearview mirror. You can imagine how tough that was on him. But he also saw Bobby climb out of the car, and when they parked everyone to clean up the track, he learned his dad was okay.

It sure didn't hurt Davey's driving. We chased him all day—before and after the wreck—and we kept up with him. But when we needed to do it—right there at the end of the race—we just didn't have enough to get around him. Still, we had a solid second place finish, less than 1 second behind Davey.

It looked to me like, if nothing else, the superspeedway side of the program was on the right track.

But that didn't make things any better in the shop and actually might have made them worse. With some people, as much as they'd like to win, they'd like to see you lose even more. We were winning, or coming close, anyway.

There was a sullen, suspicious mood around the shop, and the team was kind of split into factions. It was no fun.

Meanwhile, Darrell was calling me up and keeping after me about coming over to the Hendrick operation. Things weren't going great for him, either. Or not as great as all the "Dream Team" stuff would have had you thinking it should be going. We might not have won any races, but then they hadn't either.

I told Darrell what I'd been telling him all along—that I wasn't going to work for Waddell Wilson.

"You don't have to work for Waddell," Darrell said in one of those conversations.

"What do you mean?" I asked. It was the first time he had put it that way.

"It's not working out with him as crew chief. We're going to make a move."

"What kind of move?"

"Waddell is going to be team manager. So we'll be needing a crew chief. It would be you and me again, and with this situation here, we could win a lot of races. Win championships, too."

I asked Darrell about Rick Hendrick because I didn't know too much about him. I suppose I was suspicious of someone who came into racing from outside. But Darrell told me that Rick was the real goods, that he'd always had a love for racing, that he was a competitor, and that he wanted to win.

"You need to do this," Darrell said. "It's not going to get any better for you over there."

I couldn't argue with him about that.

Things finally came to a head between me and Brewer one night in the shop after everyone else had gone home. He'd been saying things about me to the guys on the team that had been getting back to me. I was sick of it, and I got in his face about it. We started yelling at each other, and we were about an inch from getting into it with fists, feet, and anything that was lying around handy.

I made myself back off, but it wasn't easy. I was hot.

A couple of days later, I went in to see Junior. I owed Junior a lot . . . no telling how much. And it wasn't just what I'd learned from him about racing and cars. He taught me a lot about how to be a good man, outside of racing. I remember after the 1985 season, he paid for my whole family to go up to New York for the awards dinner at the Waldorf. Not just my wife, either, but my father and mother and even my brother. Junior took care of the whole thing, and it meant a lot to me to have my family see us get that trophy, and it still does. But that was Junior. He didn't have to do it, and he didn't make a lot out of it or let me carry on about it either. He just did it.

So it was one of the hardest things I've ever done, telling Junior I was leaving, but I didn't see any other way. I told him I couldn't stay around anymore, not with things the way they were between Brewer and me. And I said I had another opportunity, with Hendrick and Darrell. Like I've said before, with Junior if you didn't want to be around, he didn't want you around.

Junior didn't yell and make a fuss, and he sure didn't beg me to stay. He wasn't that way. He just said, "Well, if that's how it is . . . "

And I said, "I guess that's how it is."

No handshakes. And especially no hugs. As much as I wanted to be out of an impossible situation, I knew I was going to miss Junior Johnson. Outside of my family, nobody had been a bigger influence or meant more to me. I felt that way then, and I feel that way now.

But you don't have a lot of time for regrets and recriminations in racing. I took my stuff and went down to Charlotte and started working for Rick. It was the first time in more than 10 years that I'd worked on a car that wasn't owned by Junior Johnson.

Some things don't change, though. In my first race with my new team—at Riverside—Darrell tangled with his old nemesis Bobby Allison in one of the S-turns. Got run clean off the track, through one of the corner stations, and scattered the people working there.

By the time Darrell got back on the track, he'd lost way too much time to make it up. I'm not saying it was intentional, but Bobby never gave anyone an inch, and he gave Darrell even less. They were rivals from back when Allison looked like he was going to win the championship and Darrell snatched it away from him.

The real story of that race was the winning driver, Tim Richmond, who was also driving a Rick Hendrick car. Richmond had been out for the first half of the '87 season. The story was still that he'd been recovering from double pneumonia. He'd come back the week before the Riverside race, at Pocono, and won there, too. So now he'd won two straight, but while the press was talking his great comeback, a lot of people in the garage area were wondering. Richmond didn't look good. There was talk about how maybe he was sicker than he was letting on or even that he was on drugs. About a month after the Riverside race, we were racing in Michigan. When it came time for him to qualify, Richmond was still in his trailer, sleeping. He got to the car with some help and managed to qualify.

Richmond started the race but blew an engine before he could finish. After the race, there were drivers who went to NASCAR and said, essentially, "Hey, we don't want to be out on the track with this guy in his condition."

Richmond made a statement about how he needed to miss a couple of more races because he had the flu or something.

He never raced again.

When he tried, at Daytona the next year, with a new ride, NASCAR insisted on a drug test. Richmond failed but not because of anything illegal. He was taking some kind of over-the-counter medication. Richmond took another test and passed, but then NASCAR wanted a look at his medical records. Richmond refused because it would have come out that he had AIDS. He sued, but NASCAR wouldn't budge. So Richmond hired a plane to drag a

banner that said, "NASCAR fans, I miss you," and it flew around the track before the start.

By then, Richmond was a pretty sick man. Less than 2 years later, he was dead. I think it hit some of us in racing harder than if he'd died on the track in a racing accident. People still talk about him, about what he was—and he was one of a kind—and what he might have done.

My own troubles, getting on track in a new operation, were nothing compared to what Richmond was going through. But I didn't know that at the time. None of us did. But I knew that when he won races in a Hendrick car, it made me want to win one, too. And I was working hard to make it happen. I was also trying hard to get used to a lot of unfamiliar ways of doing things and putting up with some resistance from Waddell Wilson. He wanted to prove that Darrell had been wrong to fire him as crew chief. If I failed, that would be the proof. So Waddell wasn't exactly helpful.

But I got support from other guys on the team, and, gradually, things started to come around. In early September at Richmond, Darrell chased Dale Earnhardt around the track and beat on his back bumper a little in the late laps, but Darrell still couldn't get by him. Still, we had a good second place finish, and we knew we could do better. Especially on the short tracks.

We got our chance 2 weeks later at Martinsville. Earnhardt was strong, again, and led from about lap 380 to 499. Darrell hung in there, though, and when we got a caution, really late, he pulled up close. When the green flag came out, it was Earnhardt, Terry Labonte, and Darrell running bumper to bumper.

Coming into the third turn, Darrell hooked Labonte's bumper, and he went into Earnhardt. While Labonte and Earnhardt were tangled up, Darrell went under both cars and won the race.

After the race, Earnhardt, of all people, started complaining, saying that Darrell should have been penalized. That first win with a new team was plenty sweet already but beating Earnhardt, and doing it that way, just made it sweeter.

I'd never really doubted that I'd made the right move. You don't look back in NASCAR, and you surely don't ever imagine that you are going back to Junior Johnson once you've left. But that win at Martinsville made me feel a lot better, and a lot more secure, about the move to Hendrick. And the team was solidly with me now. Waddell Wilson wasn't a problem, and by the next season, he was gone.

That was the only win for the "Tide Ride," in its first season. And I suppose that has to go down as a disappointment, especially after all the hoopla about the "Dream Team."

Still, we finished fourth in the points. Earnhardt won the championship. It was his second in a row and third overall. The driver we'd all known would be good from back in his dirt track days had truly arrived. I felt good for him, in a way, even though Dale and I weren't that close anymore, not after that wreck at Richmond, and now that he was a rival.

Things were about the same over at Junior's shop. Their driver, Terry Labonte, had also won one race. He was third in the points, just ahead of us. Bill Elliott was second, and Rusty Wallace was fifth. Those five looked like the teams and drivers to beat in 1988.

I figured we had a shot.

We wanted to start strong in 1988, but, of course, so does everyone else. Turned out, it was not our year to come out smoking—or maybe it was, in the literal sense. We had a very strong car at Daytona. Darrell called it, "the best car I've driven, anywhere in my life." That's high praise, even from someone who exaggerates a lot, like Darrell.

He ran strong and was out front for almost 70 laps. But the engine

(continues on page 183)

▲ Four-tire stop at Rockingham. Here I am, working out with the jack the way Junior taught me.

▼ Darrell Waltrip and I had our differences and rough times and plenty of them. But it was always all smiles in Victory Lane.

Keeping an eye on DW at North Wilkesboro.

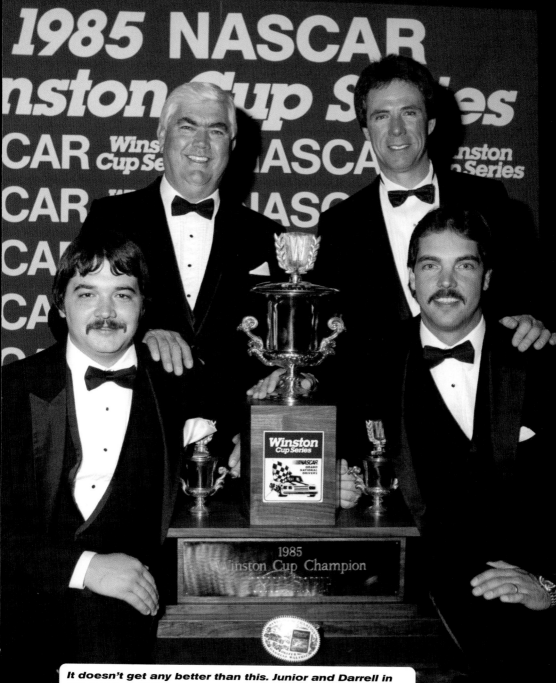

It doesn't get any better than this. Junior and Darrell in the back. Jeff Wilson, our engine builder, and me in front.

The crew celebrates by dunking me after the Tide Ride wins one at Martinsville.

▲ **With Sharon at Indy's famous Gasoline Alley in 1994. I was crew chief for Bobby Hamilton.**

▲ **Still getting it done.**

▶ **Fastest ride of my life. In 2000, I got to fly with the Air Force Thunderbirds.**

▼ **Last race as crew chief. Atlanta in 2000 with the Jack Roush team. Kurt Busch was our driver.**

New career. With Mike Joy (left) and Larry McReynolds (center)
before a Fox broadcast.

started running rough and losing power late in the race, and Darrell finished 11th. The Daytona jinx was still with him.

For the next couple of months, we had some good races, some decent races, and some disappointing races. What we didn't have was any winning races. I started aiming for Talladega, again, like I had the previous season when I was still with Junior. We built a car that I thought would run good on that track and maybe just win the race for us and give us the breakthrough we needed.

Davey Allison won the pole, but we were on the front row with him when the race started. Darrell was quick enough to lead a couple of laps before he had to quit the race, this time with a transmission problem after 83 laps.

This stuff was getting old.

We went back to Charlotte for the next race and also for another event that was even bigger than the 600. My wife, Sharon, gave birth to our first child about a week after the Talladega race. I was there for the delivery, like a lot of men are these days. And because I'd had training as an EMT, I was able to assist in the delivery. I actually brought my son, Colt Lee, into this world. It was one of those moments that you can't really describe and that you never get over.

Looking at my son in the first few minutes after he'd come into the world, I felt this huge sense of gratitude. The racing life is hard on families, with all the traveling and the late hours. But Sharon and I had hung in there, and now we had this child, and I was there for both of them at his birth. I was blessed.

The way it worked out, NASCAR is always racing in Charlotte in the month of May so I've always been around for my son's birthdays. And when our daughter was born, 16 months later, she came along in October, the other month when NASCAR is racing in Charlotte. I've missed a lot of things with the traveling, but I've been there at birthday time.

Here's a funny thing about our daughter, Heather. She was born right before a trip to Hawaii that was awarded to the crew chief whose car won the Unical Pit Crew race at Rockingham. Well, I was that crew chief, so Sharon and I were the winners of that trip. But Heather was only a couple of weeks old, and we couldn't leave her. But we weren't going to miss that Hawaii trip, either, so we loaded her up and took her with us. Whatever we did—helicopter rides, luaus—Heather did it with us. And now she can say that, unlike her brother, she has been to Hawaii. She just doesn't remember much about the trip.

I must have been in some kind of zone that May because on Memorial Day, Darrell survived in the race at Charlotte where there were 10 wrecks and beat Rusty Wallace by about two-tenths of a second. We knew tire wear was going to be a big issue in that race, and, sure enough, a lot of those wrecks were caused by blowouts. We'd been doing a lot of testing, and we knew what kind of lap times would keep our tires together longest and still keep us up near the front. We kept reminding Darrell on the radio to stick to those lap times, and he did—most of the time.

It was a wild race, and some of the wrecks were serious. Buddy Baker, one of the top veteran drivers, got a concussion that was severe enough that he eventually retired. Harry Gant, another top driver, broke his leg. So did Bud Moore, the car owner. He got run over by his own driver, Brett Bodine, in the pits. It was dangerous everywhere at Charlotte that day.

We felt really fortunate to come out in one piece, and with the win. And I was thinking that maybe it was a sign of good things to come.

But that win wasn't enough to turn things around entirely. We struggled through the summer, grinding it out and watching Elliott, Wallace, and Earnhardt win races where we thought we'd be competitive. But it seemed like we'd have a different problem every week.

We won the pole at Talladega and had the car to beat. But then we beat ourselves when the engine blew with 23 laps to go. The next week at Watkins Glen, we came even closer. This time, Darrell was leading with 4 laps to go when he had transmission problems. It was frustrating to say the very least.

We finally won a race in late September at Martinsville. It was great being back on Victory Lane, and we liked it so much we almost got there again the next week at Charlotte. This time, we couldn't get around Rusty Wallace and came in second by about a car length.

After that, we fell back among the also-rans and finished the season seventh in the points. Bill Elliott won the championship, but it was that close finish with Rusty that stayed on my mind during the off-season, I thought a lot about that race where Darrell just couldn't quite get past him, and the Charlotte race where we just barely held him off. I figured we'd be racing Rusty close and hard a lot when we got back on the track.

I sure called that one right.

*M*ost of us on the team thought that 1989 would be the year for the Tide Ride. Things had started off a little rocky in '87. We'd won just the one race, at Martinsville, a couple of months after I left Junior Johnson and came over to join up with Rick Hendrick and Darrell Waltrip. Things had gone better in '88. We'd won two races and were competitive. But we got the kind of bad breaks that can

happen to you in NASCAR. And that was also a year when Bill Elliott and Rusty Wallace were awesome.

But we thought '89 might just be our year. It was a funny thing, but after being sort of the new kid of NASCAR and challenging all the old bulls, Darrell had become a veteran, almost without realizing it. All of a sudden, this season, guys who had been around for what seemed like forever weren't there anymore. Cale Yarborough had run his last race. So had Benny Parsons and Buddy Baker. Bobby

Allison had been in a terrible wreck at Pocono and was hurt so badly he never raced again. Richard Petty was still running, but lots of people wished that he wasn't. Watching the 43 car come around down a lap or more and out of the running was like watching a boxer who'd been great once but was now long past his prime and didn't have the legs or the reflexes and was doing it on brains, memory, and guile. The fans wanted Richard to win and quit. I think his family just wanted him to quit.

So there was a new class of drivers moving up to veteran status. Along with Dale Earnhardt, Darrell was probably the most prominent among them. He'd won more races, at that time, than almost any active driver with a chance to win more. (Petty had the 200 wins, which was beyond anyone's reach, but, like I say, he wasn't a contender anymore.) We had a good shot to win any race and considered ourselves as strong contenders for the championship.

We figured we had stiff competition from Earnhardt, of course. Also Wallace and Elliott. And then there were the new "young guns." These were the drivers—and teams—that were on the verge of big things. There were always new drivers coming along, and by the time you get to the Cup circuit, you have to be good. But every now and then, you'd see something special in one of these new kids, and you'd think, "Yeah, he's got it. That kid might be the next Pearson or Petty . . . or Waltrip."

Of course, if you're Darrell Waltrip and still in your prime, you don't like hearing talk about "the new Darrell Waltrip." As far as you're concerned, *you* are still the "new Darrell Waltrip."

But that's how it is. New talent comes along. We had new drivers with old, familiar last names—Kyle Petty and Davey Allison—and we had drivers like Kenny Wallace and Alan Kulwicki, who were coming from outside of the South, which was where most NASCAR drivers had always come from. But the new veterans were not going to just roll over and let the new kids have things their way.

We knew we had a good car going down to Daytona. We thought we might even have the fastest car down there. But we got caught up in a tire switch. There was a competition during those years between Goodyear and Hoosier, a little company in Indiana that had gotten into racing in a big way. A lot of the cars that season were running on Hoosiers. We were with Goodyear.

We qualified outside pole on those tires, and then after somebody wrecked in practice because of a problem with his Goodyears, the company pulled all of its tires. We had to switch to Hoosiers. That wasn't as easy as it sounds. Matter of fact, it meant changing the whole setup of the car, and we didn't have anywhere near enough time to get it right. By race day, we knew we didn't have the car to win the race. This was going to be Darrell's 17th Daytona 500, a race he'd never won. Now it looked like that string was still not going to be broken. I'd been with Junior and Cale Yarborough for a Daytona 500 win. So I knew the feeling of winning that race, but never as crew chief. I know I wanted it as badly as Darrell did.

But you never know how you'll do. That's why they go ahead and run the races. So we were there when the man said, "Gentlemen, start your engines." It was the Daytona 500, and we were racing.

Darrell was running a good race, getting all he could out of the car, but you could tell about halfway through that we did not have a dominant car. Ken Schrader, who was also driving for Rick Hendrick, was faster than we were. So was Geoffrey Bodine, another Hendrick driver. And Earnhardt and Alan Kulwicki. We figured we'd be satisfied with a top ten or, if we got really lucky, maybe a top five.

But I was watching the race carefully—that's my job, after all—and looking at how everyone was using tires and fuel and spacing their pit stops. With around 60 laps left in the race, I started thinking that we might be able to finish without making another stop and that the guys who were ahead of us were all going to have to come in for gas. If there wasn't another caution, and we could stay out on the track, we had a chance to win this race, even though we didn't have the fastest car.

We'd be gambling. If we didn't make it on the gas we had left, it would be really embarrassing, and it could cost us a top five. But if it worked, we'd be the winners of the Daytona 500, the biggest prize of all.

Most of what I knew about racing, I'd learned from Junior Johnson. And he'd taught me that the time to gamble is when you're trying to win something. You don't take a chance and risk wrecking the car in the first 100 laps of the race when there is still time for anything to happen. But in the last laps, when the big prize is there for the taking, you put it all on the line and don't hold back.

Well, if I'd ever been in a situation like that, this was the time. So with 54 laps to go, we made our final stop. I told our gas man, Mike Powell, "Make sure you get him full. Every drop that thing will hold."

Then I told my driver what I had in mind.

"Listen, DW," I said over the radio. "After this one, I think we can make it all the way without coming in for another stop. I want you to baby that thing and make every drop of gas count."

"I don't know," Darrell said. "You really think so?"

"Yes. Stevie [Darrell's wife who was in the pit, helping us keep lap times and figure fuel mileage] does, and I do. Now let's see if we can make it happen. Get in behind any car you can and work the draft. If you can't find a car, then tuck in behind a seagull. You the man, DW. Now drive that thing."

Darrell was probably the best possible driver for that kind of situation. He was smart, and he was smooth. More than any driver of his time, Darrell was able to get on and off the throttle without wasting anything. He was never one of those guys who fought with the car, muscled it, and drove it into the ground. Darrell worked with it and tried to coax everything he possibly could out of the car. He started making extra sure that he wasn't getting on the throttle too hard or coming off of it too late. And he used every bit of the draft.

Right then, Darrell was on the lead lap and running around fifth. If the guys in front of him started dropping off to pit, and there wasn't a caution between now and the end of the race . . . well, we had a chance.

It was nail-biting time.

Kenny Schrader and Dale Earnhardt were running one and two, and with 11 laps to go, they both came in for fuel. Now we were out there with just Alan Kulwicki ahead of us. He was going to try to go the distance, too, but he'd been going a long time without a tire change. Too long. With 4 laps to go, Kulwicki blew a tire, and Darrell went into the lead.

"I don't know if we're going to make it," he said into the radio. "I'm running out of gas."

"No you're not. You're going to make it. Just baby that thing."

"I don't know."

"You're doing fine, DW. Just bring it home. You the man."

I kept talking to him like that for those last 3 laps, and they were the longest laps of my whole racing career. I kept looking for that little puff of smoke from the exhaust that you get when the car runs out of gas. I'd run the numbers over and over, and I was confident that we were going to make it. But you can't ever be sure, and there are a lot of ways to lose a race on the last lap. Every time Darrell would get on the radio and say the fuel pressure was dropping, I'd come back and say, "Shake it baby. Shake it. We want to get every drop out of that fuel cell."

I believe I probably held my breath for the whole last lap. When Darrell took the checkered flag, I was drained just as empty as his gas tank. Darrell took the cool-down lap—I was surprised he had enough gas to make it—and then we all went to Victory Lane. I had my son, who was just about a year old then, with me and my wife. I was happier than I'd ever been in racing. This was the absolute ultimate.

Somebody said later on, "You know, it must be in the numbers. It was the 17th of February, Darrell's 17th start at the Daytona 500. We were in pit number 17. And the name 'Darrell Lee Waltrip' is made up of 17 letters."

After the race, some of the other drivers and their crews were saying to us, "You know you stole that race, don't you."

"You're damned right we stole it," I told them. "And that just makes it sweeter."

After the teardown, somebody asked one of the inspectors how much gas he'd found in our fuel cell.

"I don't know, exactly," he said, "but it was little enough that for $5, I wouldn't have minded drinking it."

I was so pumped by that win that I after we'd packed everything and loaded the car on the truck, I got behind the wheel and drove all the way back to Charlotte from Daytona, that night, without stopping to sleep. I couldn't have slept if I'd tried.

Before the race and the tire problems, when we thought we had a really good chance to win, Eddie Dickerson, one of the guys on the crew, had said to me, "You know, it isn't fair. We're all working on the car, but when we win, you'll be the one who gets the Rolex watch."

That was the tradition. The crew chief of the car that won Daytona got a Rolex.

"I'll tell you what," I said. "If we win, I'll buy *you* a Rolex."

Well, it turns out that was the only year when, for some reason, they didn't follow that tradition. I didn't get a watch.

Didn't make any difference to me. I went out and bought Eddie a Rolex.

We were a winning team now. We had a long afternoon at Rockingham but came right back and beat Earnhardt out of the pits late in the race at Atlanta. That little advantage was enough for Darrell, who won the race by half a second. You just love it when you know that your good pit stop was the difference in winning the race. For the guys in the crew, that's the ultimate payoff.

We beat Earnhardt again the next month, at Martinsville, when he had air hose problems on a late pit stop, and we got in and out clean. It was getting to be a habit, and one that I liked.

We won the 600 and did it as much with strategy as anything else. We were running those Hoosier tires, and we'd tested them for how they'd hold up. We knew that if you pushed them, they'd go on you. So we figured out what the absolute optimum lap time was, to keep us racing and keep those tires from blowing. It was something like 34 seconds.

So our spotter, Randy Dorton, would time each lap. If Darrell ran faster than the 34 seconds, the spotter would call down to him and say, "Okay, back off. Pace yourself. Pace yourself."

Darrell would do it, even though it is frustrating to a driver to have cars passing him and running in front of him and not going as fast as he can. But it paid off. Some of those other cars blew right fronts and had to come to pit road. So we didn't tear up tires and knock down the wall, and when the time came, Darrell still had enough left in his tires that he could stand on it and win the race. So it was another good, smart, tactical win. We felt like we had the car, the team, and the momentum, and going into June, we were ahead in the points. We also had a shot at the Winston Million that goes to anyone who won three out of the big four races—like Bill Elliott had done in '85. We were two for two and feeling like we had a really good shot. We'd won at Daytona, after all, and Darrell had always had trouble there. He'd always run good at Talladega, the next Winston Million race.

So we took a good car and a positive attitude to Talladega, then we had a collision on pit road in the 13th lap. But Darrell wasn't anything if he wasn't a warrior. He got back in the race, and with 15 laps to go, he was leading. Terry Labonte, who was driving Junior's car, was second, and I could imagine Junior on the radio, saying, "Boy, don't you let *him* beat you." That's what he'd said to Darrell when he and Yarborough were running first and second. I know Junior wanted to beat us as badly as he'd ever wanted to beat Cale and Herb Nab. That's how it was with him.

Plus for Junior there was the added incentive of running against a Rick Hendrick car. Junior had come up strictly through racing, and it had been a hard pull. He couldn't help but look at a guy like Hendrick, who'd been really successful in business before he started his NASCAR team, as being a kind of playboy who was just buying his way in. You know, like he hadn't really earned it. And, finally, the thing with Labonte hadn't really worked out for Junior. The team never jelled, and this was their last season together. Beating me and Darrell would be a good way to end it.

When Davey Allison spun out, and we got a caution, I got a bad feeling for some reason. Might have been because it was Talladega where anything can happen and usually does. And, sure enough, Labonte got around Darrell with just 13 laps left in the race, and he stayed out front all the way to the checkered flag. That late caution, which allowed Labonte to close it up and turn it into a sprint, might have cost us the million.

But by winning almost $50,000 in the race, Darrell pushed his life-time Winston Cup winnings to more than $10 million. He was the first to do that, and it proved that Junior had been right, once again, when he saw Darrell as not just a winning driver but as a money-making driver. We left Talladega disappointed but still in the hunt for both the championship and the million.

We won at Bristol in late August, when Earnhardt spun. So we headed to Darlington the next week feeling good. Just going by the record, you had to like our chances. Darlington was a tough track, maybe the toughest, but Darrell had a good record there. One of the reasons I believe he was maybe the best pure driver to ever run in NASCAR is because he was so good on the tough tracks. He just *owned* Bristol, for instance. I'd thought Cale Yarborough had the keys to that track, but that was before I saw Darrell drive and win there.

Darrell was almost that good at Darlington.

Now when you go to Darlington, you've got a little more to worry about than usual. You're not just thinking about the competition and your car. You're thinking about the track, itself. They don't call it "The Lady in Black" or "The Track Too Tough to Tame" without a reason. I have seen more good drivers wreck there than at any other track on the circuit. When you're a crew chief at Darlington, the last thing you'll tell your driver when you're buckling him in is, "Race the racetrack."

If the car is not right, you've got to slow it down because you cannot challenge this racetrack. It will reach out and bite you. It's al-most like the track is alive and waiting, coiled up like a snake, ready to strike. There isn't a driver walking who hasn't gone down to Darlington and gotten into the wall, one time or another.

I don't know if it was Darlington or the million or maybe Darrell was remembering how years ago he'd been in a points race with Petty and come into Darlington too tight and drove too aggressively. In that particular race, Darrell hit the wall *twice* in practically the same place. Those mistakes left the door open, just enough, for Petty to come through and eventually win the points championship.

I figured that was a long time ago—10 years—and that Darrell had learned a lot since then. He was a veteran driver now with three championships and a lot more racing experience. He knew what could happen at Darlington if you got your foot too strong into the gas.

Halfway through the race, Darrell was leading and looking like he had things under control. Then Earnhardt got ahead of him, and I suppose that got Darrell's blood up. He saw that million slipping away from him, and he pressed it a little too hard. It was one of the *very* few times I saw Darrell react badly to pressure. I wouldn't say he choked, but he did feel the pressure and let things get away from him.

When he did, Darlington reached out and smacked him. He caught the wall in the fourth turn. He didn't just kiss it, either, the way you can and still keep racing. This was no "Darlington stripe" deal. He had to bring the car in so we could hammer out the quarter panel and change the tire. We lost a lot of ground and could see that million fading away. That got Darrell so mad that he came around and did it *again*, same spot, 2 laps later.

Now we had more than just body damage. He'd bent the rear-end housing and the truck arm. There were things we couldn't fix and now there wasn't any way we were going to be competitive; it was a question of survival. It was a challenge just to get the car back on the track and finish the race. We did that, but it didn't feel like much. When you finish 22nd, you don't win anything. You surely don't win a million dollars.

Darrell was philosophical about it and recited a little verse for the reporters.

"I love Darlington in the springtime. I love Darlington in the fall. I love Darlington in Victory Lane. But I hate Darlington in the wall."

A funny thing had been happening with Darrell. He had gone from being the driver fans loved to hate to a driver they just plain loved. That change had been sort of coming around for the last couple of years. I wouldn't say it was a new Darrell. Maybe just a more mature Darrell. He still ran his mouth, but a lot of the time when he did it, he was making fun of himself. He was still confident, but he wasn't arrogant. He'd won enough that he didn't have to tell everybody how good he was. Everybody knew, and there wasn't any denying it. Now he could be funny.

Earlier that season, something had happened that finally turned it all around for Darrell as far as being popular with the fans. The week before the Charlotte 600, there is a race that doesn't count for the championship points. It is also run at Charlotte, and it's called the Winston. It is an invitational race—open to winners from the previous season and qualifiers. It's generally a smaller field than normal, anywhere from 12 to 20 cars. The race is broken up into segments: seventy-five laps, then fifty, and finally ten. The first two segments determine pole position for that 10-lap sprint. The winner, back in '89, got $200,000. They came up with that format after the first two Winstons turned out to be pretty boring and didn't draw. The crowd was so thin at the second Winston that when they got ready to make the driver introductions, Darrell said, "You know, we could save a lot of time by just introducing the spectators to the drivers."

Under the new format, you had a really good chance of a free-for-all. The third year they ran it, Dale Earnhardt got into it with Geoff Bodine and then Bill Elliott and went on to win the race. On the cool-down lap, Bodine was still so mad that he ran into Earnhardt. So did Elliott, who was one of the more mild-mannered drivers in all of racing. But Earnhardt had a way of getting people's noses out of joint, and that 10-lap format brought out the old dirt-track driver in everyone.

In '89, Rusty Wallace won the first segment, and we took the second. So we were side by side, out front, for the start of the 10-lap sprint. Obviously, what you wanted to do is get out front quickly and then just hold off anybody who tried to pass you. There isn't any strategizing about pit stops and using fuel and tire wear or any of that. Just get to the front and hold on any way you can.

Well, we had the car. And Darrell went out front really quickly and was still there, coming up on the white flag. It looked like we had the thing won. Then Rusty Wallace came up under Darrell, put his nose into the left rear bumper, and spun him down into the grass. It was just about the most flagrant, intentional collision I had ever seen in racing. Still gets me mad to think about it.

We complained—bitterly—to NASCAR when they put us at the back of the pack on the restart. That did about as much good as it usually does. We started last, and Wallace won the race. We were so mad that when Rusty's team was pushing the car past us on the way to Victory Lane, one of our guys kicked it.

That was all it took. The rumble was on. Both teams were throwing punches and kicking and rolling around on the ground. There were some bloody noses and torn clothes before people got it stopped. Nobody was hurt really badly, though.

When he was interviewed after the race, Darrell said, "I hope he chokes on that $200,000."

But here is the really interesting part. The fans got all over Rusty Wallace. Booed him. Threw things at him out on the track. Just got ugly on him. And they cheered Darrell and took his side. This was happening at the same track where Darrell had challenged fans who had cheered when he wrecked to "meet in the Kmart parking lot" to settle things. Things had gone the other way so much that the fans voted Darrell NASCAR's Most Popular Driver that year and then did it again the next year. Bill Elliott won it every other year from 1984 to 2000. It was surprising that anyone could get more fan votes than Bill. And it was a real surprise that when someone did, it would be Darrell Waltrip, the driver that the fans had once loved to hate.

You talk about turning it around.

A*s great as it was for Darrell Waltrip to have been named Driver of the Year, popularity doesn't win races, or championships, and after that disappointing run at Darlington, we had our hands full trying to do both. We never really got back on our game after that race. It was sort of like the air went out of things. Maybe the distractions and disappointments of Darlington were to blame. Or*

maybe it was an idea that was starting to take shape in Darrell's mind.

There was no question that Darrell Waltrip was a successful driver. He had climbed that mountain and had more than 70 wins and $10 million in winnings to prove it. But Darrell was a deeply restless man. There was always this hunger for more. I think that's what made him so competitive. He wasn't ever satisfied with what he had. He always wanted the next challenge.

At that time, Darrell had made plenty of money driving, but he was looking around at people like Rick Hendrick, and he saw that they were making more. Rick was into a lot of things, as an owner. He was racing three teams, building engines and leasing them to other teams, and making sponsorship deals that had him making a lot of money. So I think that, in a funny way, Darrell began to feel like his competition wasn't other drivers but people like Hendrick. Darrell didn't want to be just a driver, getting paid by some owner. He wanted to be an owner/driver, competing with Rick Hendrick and Junior Johnson and making their kind of money.

By the time of that Darlington race, Darrell was thinking out loud about this. He wasn't ever one to keep quiet about what he was thinking, anyway. He'd say something to me about going off on his own and how would I like to come with him. My response was always something like, "I don't know. Maybe. We'll see."

Truth is, I was skeptical. It seemed to me that it would be taking on an awful lot. And there wasn't a strong record of success with owner/drivers. Alan Kulwicki was starting to do okay about then, and a lot of NASCAR people admired his independence and his spark. Kulwicki was from the Midwest, and he had a degree in engineering. He'd been offered a ride by no less than Junior Johnson and had turned it down to stay independent. It was a bold move, and I think that may have been a challenge to Darrell's ego, too. He heard the way people were talking about Kulwicki, and he thought, "If that kid can do it, then for sure I can do it."

Kulwicki was a good, inspirational racing story. After he won his first Cup race—at Phoenix in 1988—he took a victory lap going clockwise, the opposite direction from the way the cars raced. He called it his "Polish victory lap." The fans love it . . . and him.

But I didn't see where he was having the kind of success as an independent that Darrell and I and the rest of the team could have

with Rick Hendrick and the support we'd get from his kind of operation.

Kulwicki didn't win any races in 1989, and we finally wound up winning six. We got the last one at Martinsville, in September, but we had some problems in other races after Darlington, and we were never a threat to win the Cup. But those six wins were as many as the eventual Cup winner, Rusty Wallace, got. Dale Earnhardt, who came in second, got five. So even though we were fourth in the points race, we had as many wins as anyone. We just needed to eliminate some problems that kept us from getting the top tens and top fives, and we needed to eliminate the DNFs. Darrell and I were a lot closer, I thought, to winning our fourth championship than Alan Kulwicki was to winning his first.

But Darrell was feeling like he could do it all. We'd be back with Hendrick in '90, that looked pretty certain, but there were going to be some changes down the road, there wasn't any getting around that. So we started a new season in the kind of atmosphere of uncertainty and suspicion that I was familiar with. The difference is that when I'd been through that before, it was late in the season when we all knew a driver wasn't going to be back the next year—first, when Cale Yarborough was leaving Junior to go to M.C. Anderson and then when Darrell was running out the string before he went over to Rick's for the Tide Ride.

It wasn't a good way to end your season, and we found out that it was an even worse way to start one.

We didn't win at Daytona, in February, and by the time we got back there in July we still hadn't won. We'd had one win stolen from us, by NASCAR, at North Wilkesboro in April. They gave the race to Brett Bodine, who was a lap down when a yellow came out. When it went back to green, NASCAR put him in front. We protested, screamed and yelled, and jumped up and down, and when the dust settled, NASCAR sort of agreed with us on the facts, but they gave the win to Bodine anyway.

It was shaping up to be a long, frustrating season. You go through some like that. Everyone does, and if you've been around for a while, you learn how to handle it. I had been around long enough now and was seasoned enough to know how to get through the rough times. Everybody in any kind of professional sport eventually learns that you can't win them all. That's the first lesson. The second one is that even when you're not winning—or even having a very good year— the season goes on. There is still racing, and you've got to get the car out on the track and run the race and try to win. And if you can't win, then you try for a top five. Or a top ten. And if you can't do anything else, you just finish the race. There is a kind of code at work here. The great baseball players, in those last games of a season when their team has been out of the pennant race for weeks and weeks, still come up to the plate looking for a hit and running out ground balls to the infield. Great golfers keep on looking for birdies, grinding it out, even when they've barely made the cut and don't have a chance of winning the tournament. That's what you do when you are a professional. It's about pride.

Everyone on the team was frustrated because we weren't winning. But nobody was phoning it in. We were still working hard in the garage between races, trying to make the car run faster. And we were still trying to make the cleanest, quickest stops possible in the pits. We didn't quit—not even when Darrell crashed at Daytona and got hurt so badly he couldn't drive for six races.

The crash didn't even occur during a race; it was in practice. That's the kind of season it was.

Darrell was out with some other drivers, working on drafting, right at the end of practice when Terry Labonte had something come loose and spilled oil all over the track. Darrell got into that spilled oil and spun. While Darrell was spinning, Dave Marcis came through the melee and caught him hard—just T-boned him—right in the driver's side door.

I called Darrell on the radio, and when he didn't answer, I went running down there. He was awake by the time I got to him, but he was in bad shape. He'd had his bell rung, just like the last time he'd wrecked at Daytona, but he also had a really badly broken leg. I kept talking to him, telling him he'd be okay, while they cut him out of the car and put him in the ambulance to take him to the hospital.

Now I had to make up my mind. Was I going to the hospital with him, or was I going to stay there at the track and do my job?

I stayed at the track and did my job.

We worked on making the backup car ready, and I got Jimmy Horton to drive in relief for us. When I'd gotten those things under control, I went to the hospital to see Darrell. His leg was broken so badly they had to do surgery to put a rod in. He was pretty depressed about that. It had been a long time since he'd missed a race.

Darrell missed a lot more of them that season. But the team kept it together, and we made the car as good as we possibly could, every week, for whoever we got to drive. We didn't win, but we didn't embarrass ourselves either. We were racing for pride.

Darrell came back, at Pocono, with his leg still not healed and tried to drive. We had to lift him into the car. He made one lap and realized how dangerous it was, trying to race in his condition, and he brought the car into the pits. We lifted him out and went with a relief driver.

It was the first year since 1974 that Darrell Waltrip didn't win a single Cup race. But even though we didn't make it to Victory Lane, the car still finished in the top ten. Even with the different drivers—all of them just utility guys, no stars among them—the distractions, and the real concern we all felt about Darrell, we still had a decent season. Not great, but decent. And that year may have been when I did some of my best work, keeping the team together, keeping everybody focused, and keeping us respectable.

By the end of that season, it was pretty clear the way things were going. Even before he was able to start driving again, Darrell was working on setting up his own team for the next year. He was talking to potential sponsors and lining things up. His deal with Rick Hendrick was clearly over and the mood between the two of them was about like it had been between Junior and Darrell at the end of their time together.

Cold. Really cold.

Darrell was talking to me about coming to work for him, and I still wasn't sure that was the smart way for me to go. So I went in and talked to Rick about it.

"You got anything for me here?" I asked.

Rick is a smart guy who sees a long way past the next thing that's coming. He looks way, way down the road.

"You know," he said, "you two have got something together. You're one of the great teams. You can put up with him and get things out of him that nobody else can. And I think maybe you ought to keep that combination together."

I took it as a compliment and sincere advice from somebody I respected. There would be times, though, when I'd wonder. I see Rick all the time, but I've never asked him if he was telling me what he believed or if he just wanted to get rid of me.

Either way, that off-season I was building a new operation from scratch. We started out in the garage with four bare walls. I believe it was the hardest I'd ever worked, in the whole time I'd been in racing. We had to do everything, right down to hanging Sheetrock. We didn't own a toolbox when we started, and Darrell Waltrip Motorsports was going to be racing in 1991 with Western Auto for a sponsor.

Somehow, we got it done, and when the season started, Darrell had the old fire. It took us a little while to shake the bugs out, but in late April we won the seventh race of the season at North Wilkesboro. Darrell got across the finish line about 1 second ahead of Dale Earnhardt. It was the first race we'd won in almost 2 years—19 months to be exact—and it felt like maybe the really bad times were behind us, and that this new deal was going to work out.

This was one of those races that, once you've won it, what you feel is *relief*. The load has been lifted, and now you can get back to racing.

We managed one more win that season, at Pocono. Got by Earnhardt, again. So that was sweet, and maybe it was a little sweeter at the end of the season when Dale won the Cup. With a whole new operation that we'd put together in just about 3 months, we were able to win two races, take a top ten in 17 others, and finish eighth in the points. And we'd outraced the Cup winner in two races.

There was still a lot of uncertainty about this new operation, but things were definitely looking promising.

The next season, though, things started going wrong in little ways that just kept growing bigger. We were struggling and hadn't won a race by about mid-season, and I could tell that Darrell was getting frustrated. We were all getting frustrated. And there were some other things going on in Darrell's life. He'd never been one of the really big hell-raisers in racing, but he'd had his good times. Now he'd found religion and accepted Christ, and he was a family man. He was thinking about things a little differently and listening to a lot of people who weren't in racing and didn't know anything about racing.

Well, one day, without any discussion or warning, Darrell named a new "team manager" to be the guy in charge of everything. I was still the crew chief, but I was supposed to answer to this new man, whose name is Sam Conway. He'd never been in racing, and he didn't know anything about racing. He'd been a success at making dentures.

But Conway was the boss, and he let everyone know it, including me. He told me that he was looking at the whole operation, starting from the top down, and that meant he had his eye on me. I almost went over the desk after him. Then he told me that if I wanted to communicate with Darrell, I was supposed to do it through him.

The next time I saw Darrell, at the track, I let him have it. I told him exactly what I thought about his new arrangement and how it was going to work.

"Calm down, take it easy," he said. "It's going to be all right. You just need to understand what we're trying to do."

Darrell never really explained what that was, and I'm not sure he knew himself. Maybe he thought he needed someone to run the operation more like a business and less like an old-fashioned racing team. It didn't make any sense to me then, and it still doesn't now.

The way that conversation ended, I told Darrell that as long as I worked for him and cashed his checks, I'd be giving him 100 percent. But I told him that I didn't think this new arrangement was going to last very long and that if it started going down, I wasn't going to stick around and go down with it.

We sort of agreed to disagree.

I knew I couldn't work for Sam Conway, so I went to talk to Rick Hendrick. I asked him the same question I'd asked him before.

"You got anything for me?"

He didn't. But through Rick, I got into some discussions with Felix Sabates, who was a guy who came to America from Cuba without a dime and had a lot of success in business. Felix had gotten into racing with Kyle Petty driving his number 42 car, and now he wanted to bring a new, young driver named Kenny Wallace up from the Busch circuit and into Cup racing. He thought he needed an experienced crew chief and was I interested?

"I'll let you know," I told him.

He wanted an answer, but he agreed to give me a little time.

We had a race coming up at Pocono, the track where Darrell had last won a race. We had built a good car for that race, and things were coming around in spite of Sam Conway. So I thought I'd just see how things went with that race before I made up my mind.

Well, we ran good, and Darrell won the race. You'd have thought that Sam Conway was driver, crew chief, engine man, tire man, and spotter all rolled into one. I watched the way he was, and I knew that there was just no way I could stay around with that situation.

So I quit a winner, left Darrell Waltrip Motorsports, and signed on with Felix Sabates's Dirt Devil team. It wasn't exactly the way I'd wanted things to work out. I'd gone with Darrell when he wanted to be an owner, even though I wasn't sure it was the smart thing to do. And I'd hung in for the first tough months and got us to where we were winning races. You don't like to leave something you've built.

Also, Darrell and I had been through a lot together. It was at the point now with us where we were talking in a kind of code sometimes. We just knew each other that well. Like I've said, Darrell was known around racing as one of the more difficult drivers to deal with, but I had worked it out. I could hear what he was saying when a lot of other people heard just angry words. I knew when to give it back to him and when to take it. I knew how to calm him down, and I knew when to praise him. We had won a lot of races together, and it was a real partnership and not just a business deal.

So emotionally, it wasn't easy.

But as a business deal, it was a no-brainer. Darrell liked money, and he always wanted to make more. That's why he kept changing rides, even when he was on top, and why he eventually went with owning his own team. He didn't like the idea that there was anybody in racing making more money than Darrell Waltrip.

But he wasn't exactly throwing money around, once he became a team owner. I'd been in NASCAR a long time by now, since before the really big money started showing up in the sport after live television and when racing broke out of just being a regional, Southern thing. I'd done all right, but I'd never gotten rich the way some guys had by going with some new start-up operation that wanted to buy itself a winner, really fast.

I'd actually gone with Darrell out of loyalty. It sure wasn't the money. But with Felix, it was both a good opportunity with a promising young driver and, also, it was the money. Not long after I told Darrell I was leaving, I was interviewed on a radio show. I told the host, "You know, I believe that my ship has finally come in, and it's an aircraft carrier."

Darrell Waltrip won two more races that year, with cars I'd built for him. Those were the last NASCAR races he ever won. In his career, Darrell won 84 races. That puts him fourth on the all-time list. I was his crew chief for 43 of those races. We were one of the most successful partnerships in NASCAR history, and I wouldn't trade anything for that.

The winner in the points that year was Alan Kulwicki. This proved that an owner/driver could do it. And it must have been hard on Darrell that the owner/driver who did it wasn't him. I'm sure it made him just that much more determined to make it work, even when everything was screaming to him that it wasn't working.

Alan Kulwicki, by the way, never got the chance to defend his championship. He was killed in an airplane crash a couple of months into the next season. He was one of the real rising stars in NASCAR, and it was one of several tough losses that seemed to come really quickly, one after another. First, Clifford Allison—Davey's younger brother—was killed in New Hampshire, practicing for a Busch series race. Then, not long after the Kulwicki airplane crash, Davey Allison was flying a helicopter and something went wrong. Those were three young men with terrific potential, and, suddenly, they were all gone. You know when you get into it that racing is a dangerous sport. But these young drivers hadn't died during races. Two of them hadn't even died in cars. There was a feeling around the sport during those months that we were living under some kind of a cloud.

The '93 season was the first one in a long time where Darrell Waltrip and I weren't together for a single race. We'd gone our separate ways and—while probably neither of us would have said so then—our best days in racing were behind us. There were other combinations coming along that were going to experience the same kind of glory we'd had in our time.

In 1993, a rookie driver came along and right away he reminded you of Darrell Waltrip in the way he drove—smooth, instinctive, and artistic—even if he didn't have the big mouth. You only had to see Jeff Gordon drive once or twice to know that he was the real goods and that he was going to Victory Lane—many, many times.

Gordon was coming on strong in Cup racing at exactly the time when Dale Earnhardt was at his peak as a driver, winning the points in '93 and again in '94. That made a total of seven championships for Earnhardt, which tied him with Richard Petty. I think most NASCAR fans expected him to pass the King and maybe even win 10 before he retired.

At that point in his career, Dale was still driving aggressively. But he was also driving smart. He and his owner, Richard Childress, made a great team, and that black number 3 car was the favorite of millions of NASCAR fans. Dale was their kind of driver, and to them he represented the pure roots of stock car racing. He was the real deal.

Those traditional NASCAR fans considered Gordon an outsider and a threat, not just to win races but to somehow . . . I don't know, *steal* something from them. Gordon was a California kid who looked even younger than he was. He was good-looking, in a very clean-cut way, and very polite. He was about as far in looks and manners as you could get from the old, whiskey-running, hard-charging, redneck driver who was the early image of the sport. Dale Earnhardt, in the mind of the fans, was the legitimate heir of that tradition.

Jeff Gordon was an outsider and an interloper, and the fans plain didn't like him. They felt the same way about Gordon that they had about Darrell back when he came along and was knocking off Richard Petty and Cale Yarborough.

But there wasn't any question about Gordon's driving. Of course, if he hadn't been a great driver, he wouldn't have been a threat. The fan's hatred was, in a way, a sign of respect.

Gordon won his first championship in 1995, driving for Rick Hendrick, who was bringing him along the year after Darrell and I left. He won again in 1997 and 1998. Then again in 2001.

Dale never won that eighth championship, and, of course, he never will.

While Hendrick and Gordon were on the way up, Darrell's owner/driver deal was going in the other direction. In 1996, he talked me into coming back at about the middle of the season. I'd moved from Sabates back to Darrell's operation and things were going okay, but I guess I had the idea that maybe Darrell and I could bring back the old magic. We had once been the best, and it is hard to admit—or even to know—that your time has passed. I looked at what Gordon and his crew chief, Ray Everham, had going, and it made me think of those championship years with Darrell. So I decided to try and turn back the clock.

We didn't win any races in the half-season I was with the team, but I felt like we were making progress. At the end of the season, Darrell said he was satisfied and was looking forward to next year. I said I was, too.

I went to the team Christmas party, and Darrell gave me a hug and a bonus check. That party was on a Sunday. He fired me on Monday with no explanation except to say that he'd changed his mind and "wanted to go in a different direction."

This time, I said, it was forever. And it was. As driver and crew chief, anyway. I wasn't going to get into a Billy Martin/George Steinbrenner kind of deal with Darrell. So we had a real shouting match, and I walked out, figuring it was the last I'd ever speak to him. I went off to do some consulting and eventually get back into racing for the Jack Roush operation. I was crew chief for Chad Little for a while and then for Kurt Busch in his first seven Winston Cup races. That was in 2000, my last year on pit lane.

Darrell, meanwhile, continued to struggle as an owner/driver. The business wasn't doing so good, and the racing was worse. A lot of people in racing wanted him to quit. Seeing him out there, running two or three laps down without a chance to win was like watching Petty in his last few seasons when he had no chance to win and was being passed by guys who would have been trying to get out of his way when he was in his prime.

The sport had been getting younger, and the reason for that was mostly because of marketing. If you were going to put together a winning NASCAR operation in the late '90s, you needed heavy sponsorship and backing. Sponsors wanted the new, youthful image, and they wanted to believe that they were getting in on the ground with something that was new and growing. The veteran drivers could still compete, but they were familiar and stale. They were, inevitably, going to decline and leave the sport.

Don't get me wrong. There were still plenty of veteran drivers around, and some of them were doing all right. Dale Jarrett comes to mind. And Mark Martin. But the excitement and the energy in NASCAR was—and is—with the "young guns." The whole movement in NASCAR was in that direction, and it wasn't long before Jeff Gordon was one of the established stars, fighting off new guys like Tony Stewart, Dale Earnhardt Jr., and Kurt Busch.

I believe that in the late '90s—when Darrell was struggling and fans were wishing that he'd just go ahead and hang it up—he could still drive, and he would have won races and been up there in the points if he'd had a good ride. He hadn't lost that much—Harry Gant won races when he was in his fifties—but he didn't have the operation around him that he needed. And as owner/driver, he was never going to get it. The action and energy was with owners like Hendrick, Roush, and Childress. Darrell's decline on the track was almost a corporate thing, in my opinion, and not a driving thing.

But that's how it is in racing. The end of a great driver's career usually isn't very pretty.

Dale Earnhardt stayed competitive after he'd won his last championship in 1994. He came back from way down and almost caught Gordon in '95. Everybody in NASCAR, it seemed like, was pulling for him to do it. They weren't happy about the changing of the guard. Dale was fourth in '96. And in '97, even though he was fifth, he didn't win a race. Some people thought this was the beginning of the end and were praying that he didn't go out like Petty. That kind of end just didn't seem right when you were talking about Dale Earnhardt. The Intimidator is supposed to go out with a bang, not a whimper.

That's why the 1998 Daytona 500 was one of the greatest races in NASCAR history and one of my best racing memories. It was NASCAR's 50th anniversary season and the 20th time Dale had run in the biggest race of all. He hadn't won a race in 59 starts, and I don't think anyone—except Dale, himself—expected him to win that one.

So he went out and ran a great race. Led the last 60 laps and beat Bobby Labonte. After Dale took the checkered flag, he drove down pit row where the people from every crew had lined up like some kind of honor guard. As he came by, he was giving high fives. I was standing there, with all the other guys from the crews, and it was a great moment for me when I gave a high five to my old friend, after maybe the biggest win of his career.

That was the only win Dale got that year. He came back in '99 and won three races. Then in 2000, he won two more and climbed all the way back to second in the points. So maybe he wasn't done yet.

Darrell and I were nearly there. We were both in our last season of racing. Darrell had been out of the owner/driver business for a couple of seasons now. He had sold everything in '98 and was driving for people like Tim Beverly and Travis Carter, who'd been on Junior's team with me and was now an owner but not a really successful one. Not like Rick Hendrick, anyway, who had Gordon and other big-time drivers and where Darrell could probably have still been driving and winning if he hadn't had that hunger for more. Probably the brightest spot in a pretty dark time was when Darrell ran a couple of races as a relief driver for Earnhardt's team. It must have been hard on his pride, but the truth is—first, last, and always—

Darrell Waltrip was a driver, and he wanted to drive. So he took the best ride he could get and went out on the track and raced.

But 2000 was the end of the racing trail for both of us. Darrell was still very popular with the fans and already had a lot of outside stuff going on, including some broadcasting. I was doing a little radio, myself. I had a show called *NASCAR Country* that covered racing and country music. I did interviews with drivers and musicians and some racing analysis. The show was syndicated to about 100 stations around the world. It had started out as kind of a sideline deal, but I was getting more and more interested in it.

NASCAR had decided, at about this time, that it was going to bundle all of the television coverage together, into one package. Up to now, there had been several different arrangements with various networks and cable companies. NASCAR was looking to negotiate a package. A very big package.

When all the dust settled, there were two outfits left standing—FOX and NBC—and the price tag was in the billions. The other outfits that had been doing NASCAR—ESPN, ABC, and TNN—would do their last broadcasts in 1999.

When FOX was putting together its broadcasting team, it went to Darrell for an on-the-air color job. He'd been doing some of that for cable, and he was good at it and popular with the fans. Darrell was finally moving out of racing into a new career where his talking would only be an asset.

The people who were putting together the FOX team asked him about somebody for the job of studio analyst. Much to my surprise, Darrell and Van Colley, his business manager, recommended me.

I got a call to come in and do a test. This was in May of 2000 when I was still with the Roush operation. I was nervous, but I must have done all right because in July they called me back and offered me the job.

I went to Jack and told him I'd had an offer and, to be honest, to feel him out about what my future was with his operation. I don't know if I was burned out, exactly, but I had been working in the pits since I was a teenager and was thinking that maybe it was time for a change. Racing is a demanding profession, and I had been doing it for a long time. Maybe it was time to get out of the pits and spend a little more time with the family.

But I wasn't sure that I was ready to hang it up or if the broadcasting thing was the right way to go. I knew I was a good crew chief. I still wasn't sure about being on television. The truth is, the idea of it was a little intimidating.

Jack told me he thought it was a great opportunity and that he knew I'd be good at it. And that is what I needed to hear. I called FOX and told them yes. My first race would be the Daytona 500 in February. I finished out that year with Jack Roush. He moved Kurt Busch over from the truck series and into the car Chad Little had been driving. We had some good races but, unfortunately, no wins. It would have been good to go out with one more trip to Victory Lane.

So Darrell and I were back together. There are some teams that just can't be broken up, I guess. I'd thought that after the last divorce, when he'd fired me after giving me a bonus check at the Christmas party, we wouldn't ever have anything to do with each other again. But we didn't stay mad at each other very long. There had been too many good times, too much success, to let that bad stretch at the end poison it all. I was glad to be working with him again.

The first race we did for FOX was the one at Daytona where Dale Earnhardt hit the wall on the last lap and died from his injuries. I think most of us in racing knew, when we saw how hard the car hit and the way Kenny Schrader starting waving for the crew, that it was bad and probably as bad as it could possibly be. When I saw the crew cutting the roof off the car, I had the same feeling I'd had way, way back when I was a kid, watching the race at Charlotte when Fireball Roberts's car crashed and caught on fire.

You know when you get into racing that it is a dangerous game. You lose friends, and that's inevitable. But even after you lose Tim Richmond, Alan Kulwicki, and Davey Allison, you aren't prepared when Dale Earnhardt is killed. I still think back on the times when we were both still young and just getting started in racing and were competitors on the track and friends off of it, and I miss him.

Looking back on those days, from where I am now, it is sometimes hard to believe how far racing has come and how much it has changed. The money is so much bigger, and the technology is so much more sophisticated. The appeal of the sport has grown so far past the old, rural roots that there is now only one sport in America that is more popular—professional football. Millions and millions of people are NASCAR fans. When I started, there was maybe 2 hours of tape-delayed coverage of the Daytona 500 on television. This year, FOX will do almost 100 hours of live coverage of Speedweeks alone. Daytona is now right up there with the Super Bowl as an American carnival.

If you go up to Wilkes County, you'll see that a section of highway 421 has been named for Junior Johnson. This is the road he once drove down hauling liquor. I think that probably says it all about how far racing has come. The old renegades have become legendary heroes.

Big as it has gotten, racing is still about the cars and the drivers and the crews. It is about trying to go faster than the other guy and doing what you have to do to keep him from getting past you on the last lap. It is about drafting at Daytona, swapping paint at Bristol, and trying not to get into the wall at Darlington. It is about the gaudy paint schemes in the sponsor's colors and the infield packed with fans

wearing their driver's colors and drinking the sponsor's beer. It is about a voice—maybe even the President's voice—coming over the loudspeaker with the words, "Gentlemen, start your engines." It is about making good, clean pit stops and going hard for the checkered flag and riding into Victory Lane with your fist in the air.

Racing has changed, but a lot of it is still the same and will never change. The things about racing that got me into it when I was just a kid keep me coming back, 30 years later. Once it gets in your blood, it never leaves.

These days, I live in a house that's an hour away from the one where I grew up. But sometimes at night, if the wind is right and I'm lying in bed, trying to go to sleep, I swear I can hear them coming around turn four at the track in Charlotte, just like I could when I was a boy and racing was still a dream.

INDEX